French
Provincial Cooking

French
Provincial Cooking

Tony Schmaeling

OMEGA BOOKS

Acknowledgements

A lot of people have helped me in putting together this, the first in a series of international cookbooks.

I'd like to thank Kevin Weldon, former Managing Director of Paul Hamlyn who started it all. Warwick Jacobson and Helen Frazer of Hamlyns also gave me their wholehearted encouragement and support.

My thanks to Graham Turnbull at Traveland whose company made it possible for me to travel to Europe in style and comfort. Graham's secretary Melinda was also very helpful and I'm grateful to her.

The generosity and organization of the French Tourist Bureau made my trip through France pleasant and efficient and I thank the various officers for their unstinting help: Monsieur Jean Francois Houdin in Sydney, Madame Stadelmann in Frankfurt, Madame Rieffel in Strasbourg and especially Madame Andrieux in Paris who not only looked after me while I was there but, on my return, sent me additional recipes and various pieces of clothing which I'd forgotten.

Angela Crammond gave me invaluable help in research and translation and Gwen and Michelle Flanders typed up reams of my almost indecipherable longhand.

Susan Tomnay, my editor, had the hardest job of all. Without her perseverance and humour I couldn't have done it.

Paul Ring travelled with me through France and, within the space of a few days, became a very proficient camera assistant. I thank him.

Finally it would be remiss of me not to mention the inspiration and technical background I have derived from Waverley Root's magnificent book 'The Food of France'.

Photography by Tony Schmaeling and Reg Morrison

Designed by Warren Penney Edited by Susan Tomnay

Contents

THE PROVINCES OF
FRANCE

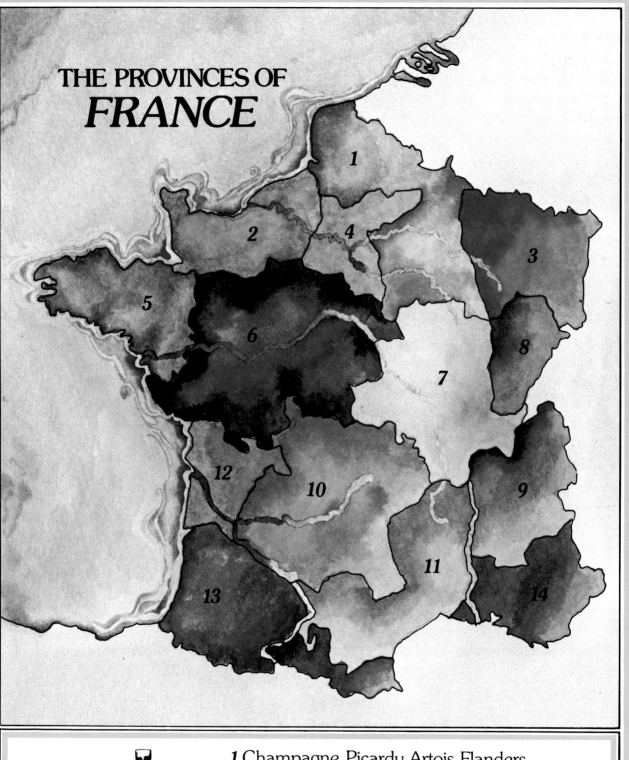

1 Champagne, Picardy, Artois, Flanders
2 Normandy *3* Alsace-Lorraine *4* Ile-de-France
5 Brittany *6* The Loire Valley *7* Burgundy
8/9 Franche-Comté, Savoy, Dauphiné
10/11 The Central Plateau and Languedoc
12 Bordeaux *13* Western Pyrenees
14 Provence, Côte d'Azur

Introduction

The many faces and facets of France are reflected in the great variety of its food.

Gastronomically, the country as we see it today is made up of many provinces which in the past, in one way or another, have lead their own existences as independent counties or dukedoms or even as sovereign kingdoms.

That is why, when we speak of French food, we think of the food of the different provinces: Alsace with its fois gras, Normandy its dairy products and apples etc. Even haute cuisine, refined through the ages by the chefs of the aristocracy, has provincial origins.

For me, the most interesting aspect of French cooking is that it is a living and ever-growing thing. During my travels through France, having done a great deal of reading on French food, I would arrive at my destination in any province where I was to collect recipes and take photographs of regional dishes, expecting some typical examples which would best represent the region. Not so, because for the chef to present just a standard rendition of a local dish would be considered an insult to his culinary 'genius'.

Every cook, every chef, be it at home or in a public eating place, makes his or her own contribution to the ever changing and growing cuisine of the country.

This does not mean that there is no bad food in France. Alas, even here they have their share of it. Escoffier would turn in his grave if he saw the fast-food places along the Champs Elysées.

But at every stop I made in France, I saw examples of that personal touch and the proud announcement of it on the menus. 'Fait à la maison', 'à la façon du chef', 'préparé par le chef', or proclaiming the name of its creator: 'la Truite Soufflée 'Celine'', 'Rognon de Veau Flambés 'Lasserre'' and countless others.

There is hardly any other country where travelling "by one's stomach" is more fun. There is always the element of pleasant surprise and discovery, and for the connoisseur, there's the satisfaction of finding yet another 'gem' of provincial food.

In this book I have tried to put together a medley of recipes, many of them collected during my gastronomic tour through the provinces of France. Some of those selected are included because they are representative of the food from that province, but most of them are here because they are interesting, fun to prepare and great to eat. A large number of these recipes was very kindly and unstintingly given to me by the chefs or owners of the many restaurants I visited. They also prepared the fine food which I photographed and which I hope in some way conveys the different feelings and atmospheres of their establishments.

I didn't spend nearly as long in France as I would have liked, but despite my hurried progress, I was able to take in what I consider to be the very essence and spirit of French cooking: the rich diversity of the dishes, the ability of French cooks to get the best out of local ingredients, and, even in the most modest dishes, the evidence of an attitude to cooking which few people in other countries possess.

I hope that I can pass on to the reader my own enthusiasm for French cooking, and that the cooks who will use these recipes will derive as much pleasure as I have had, collecting, putting them together, and finally preparing them and savouring the results.

I have always maintained that the hardest, most complicated dish, properly described, can be prepared by anybody with a reasonable understanding of cooking. Therefore my style of describing the method is a clear and succinct series of instructions enabling even an inexperienced cook to try his or her own 'genius'.

This leads me back to my previous remarks about 'genius'. All recipes can be added to and changed and I consider this one of the most appealing aspects of French cooking. I know hardly any French chef or cook who slavishly follows a recipe. The French change their cooking according to the season, and use recipes which incorporate a particular seasonal product, but when they decide on a dish, and an ingredient needed for it is not available, they improvise.

This ability and willingness to improvise is their 'genius'. So please attack this book with enthusiasm and without any trepidation, use your 'genius' and when in doubt, IMPROVISE. BON APPÉTIT!

Tony Schmaeling

NOTE
All flour used in this book is plain (all-purpose) flour, unless otherwise specified.

Alsace-Lorraine

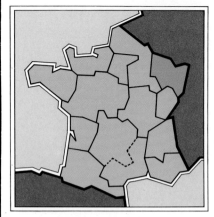

It is customary to bracket the name Alsace-Lorraine, but only in name is it a unit. Their food and their culture have developed along quite different lines.

Alsace stands strongly under the influence of Germany. Its architecture and folklore are more like those of the people of the Black Forest across the river Rhine. And so is its food: sausages, dumplings, noodles and sauerkraut echo the cooking of Germany. And of course, the goose, the festive bird of Germany and its foie gras are invariably associated with the cuisine of Alsace.

While foie gras was known to the Romans, it was in the 18th Century that the modern version is said to have been invented by the chef to the governor of Alsace. Other regions of France claim it as their own too, and in almost any part of the country chefs swear that it is a speciality of their town. So much so, that on my tour through France collecting material for this book, the signature saying of the trip became 'not foie gras again!' Good hearty wholesome food is the main gastronomic characteristic of Alsace. It is certainly not haute cuisine, but it is farmhouse cooking at its best. Indeed the local farmers take a great deal of pride in displaying their prosperity and the quality of their food is one way of showing it.

One of the most interesting ways to see the area is by following the 'wine route'. It starts at Strasbourg, the gateway to all parts of Alsace and leads along the hilly vineyards which produce the great wines of Alsace. The traveller will pass through many romantic mediaeval villages whose architecture is so like that of Germany.

Lorraine, situated between Alsace and the Île-de-France, is influenced by them both. There are not many distinctive regional dishes and even these are to a large extent derived from the classical cuisine of the Île-de-France.

The exception is of course the Quiche Lorraine. Its fame has spread throughout the world where its original form of a round delicate pastry flan filled with pieces of bacon and a cream-egg custard is reproduced with varying degrees of success.

The region is well known for its sweets. Nancy has its Macaroons, while Commercy is famous for its Madeleines. The great Alsacian Gewurtz Traminers, Silvaners and Rieslings, fresh and fruity in character, complement a fine cuisine. Nancy, the capital of Lorraine, has one of the most beautiful planned urban spaces in France. Built by Stanislas Leczinski, Duke of Lorraine, ex-King of Poland and father-in-law of Louis XV, it is a progression of squares joining the Place Royal and the Government Place. It is a delightful place to visit, both from the architectural point of view and because there are some excellent restaurants there.

Between Alsace and Nancy is Baccarat, where the famous and exquisite crystal is made. Mineral water is made at Vittel and some of the best beer in France is brewed at Metz.

Misty scene, Alsace area

Foie Gras d'Oie Frais

Fresh goose liver
This recipe comes from the Restaurant Buerehiesel in Strasbourg.

Serves 4-6

600-900 g (1¼-1¾ lb) fine goose livers
salt and freshly ground black pepper

1. Preheat the oven to 160°C (325°F).
2. Remove any sinews from the livers. Season with salt and pepper.
3. Fit the livers tightly into a terrine, taking care not to crush them.
4. Cover the terrine, stand in a dish of boiling water and place in the oven.
5. Cook for 1½ hours.
6. Allow to cool, and keep in the refrigerator for 3 to 4 days before serving.
7. Cut into slices with a knife which has been dipped in hot water, or serve with a spoon.

Quiche Lorraine

Alsace-Lorraine is the home of the quiche, and each village has its own recipe for this popular hot cheese pie. Traditionally, Quiche Lorraine is made with diced fat, salt pork or green bacon, but there can be any number of variations on the basic theme, using mushrooms, crab, zucchinis and so on.

Serves 4–6

short pastry for a 20 cm (8 in) pie
** (see p. 150)**
4 egg yolks plus 1 whole egg, beaten
1¼ cups (10 fl oz) cream
salt and freshly ground black pepper

grated nutmeg
125 g (4 oz) green bacon or speck, in
** one piece**
30 g (1 oz) butter
125 g (4 oz) Gruyère, diced

1. Preheat the oven to 190°C (375°F).
2. Prepare the pastry and line a pastry tin or quiche dish with it.
3. Prick the bottom with a fork, brush with a little beaten egg and bake blind for 15 minutes.
4. Whisk the egg yolks in a bowl.
5. Add the cream and whisk until thick and lemon coloured.
6. Season to taste with salt, pepper and nutmeg.
7. Cut the green bacon or speck into thin strips, and remove the rind.
8. Blanch the bacon pieces in boiling water for 3 minutes.
9. Melt the butter in a small pan and sauté the bacon gently until golden.
10. Arrange the diced bacon and the cheese in the pastry case.
11. Pour over the cream and egg mixture and bake for about 30 minutes or until golden brown on top.
12. Serve immediately.

Filet de Sandre aux Nouilles Fraîches

Fillet of Sandre with fresh noodles
Any firm, white fleshed fish may be used. This recipe comes from the Restaurant
Buerehiesel in Strasbourg.

Serves 6

3 spring onions (scallions),
  finely chopped
1.25 kg (2½ lb) firm fleshed fish fillets,
  such as kingfish, snapper, etc.
salt and freshly ground black pepper

1 cup (8 fl oz) Riesling
1 cup (8 fl oz) + 2 tablespoons cream
1 cup (8 fl oz) fish fumet (see p. 149)
100 g (3½ oz) butter

1. Preheat the oven to 180°C (350°F).
2. Arrange the finely chopped spring onions in a flameproof dish.
3. Lay the fish fillets on the top.
4. Season with salt and freshly ground black pepper.
5. Moisten with the white wine, the two tablespoons of cream and the fumet.
6. Bring this liquid to the point of boiling, then transfer the dish to the oven for 6 to 8 minutes to simmer until cooked.
7. When the fish fillets are cooked, arrange them on a bed of fresh cooked noodles and keep them warm.
8. Reduce the cooking liquid over a high flame until it is half the original volume.
9. Add the remaining cream, and then, little by little, the butter, whisking well with a wire whisk to blend the sauce.
10. Check the seasoning, and pour over the fish fillets and noodles.
11. Return to a hot oven for a couple of minutes before serving piping hot.

Nouilles Fraîches

Fresh Noodles from the Restaurant Buerehiesel in Strasbourg.

Serves 6

5 cups (1¼ lb) flour
6 eggs

1 teaspoon salt
a dash of white wine

1. Mix the flour, eggs, salt and a little wine in a bowl.
2. When the dough is well blended, divide it into six pieces.
3. Allow the dough to rest for ½ hour covered with a damp cloth.
4. Then stretch each of the six pieces of dough out finely with your hands.
5. Allow them to dry for about 15 minutes.
6. Re-fold each piece of dough many times, stretching and folding, until finally it is thin and elastic.
7. Cut the dough into little strands with a knife.
8. The noodles should be cooked in boiling, salted water for 5 minutes, or until cooked.

Les Écrevisses Pattes Rouge à la Nage

Freshwater Crayfish Tails in Bouillon
This recipe comes from the Capucin Gourmand in Nancy.

Serves 4

3 cups (24 fl oz) Chablis or any good
   quality dry white wine
6 spring onions (scallions), chopped
4 carrots, sliced
½ stick celery, cut into 2½ cm
   (1 in) lengths
1 tablespoon tarragon, chopped

1 fennel bulb, chopped into
   small pieces
½ small hot red pepper
12 peppercorns
½ teaspoon salt
8 crayfish or king prawns

1. Combine all the ingredients except the crayfish and gently simmer for half an hour.
2. Add the crayfish and simmer for about 3 minutes.
3. Remove the tails and peel them.
4. Arrange two per person in the bottom of a soup bowl. Taste the bouillon and if necessary add more salt or pepper.
5. To serve, pour the bouillon over the crayfish.

Filet de Turbot au Beurre Rouge

Fillet of turbot with red butter sauce
Where turbot is not available, fillets of flounder may be substituted. This recipe comes from the Restaurant Capucin Gourmand in Nancy.

Serves 4

1 bottle of Burgundy (red)
1.5 kg (3 lb) turbot fillets (or flounder)
125 g (4 oz) butter, chilled

¼ cup (2 fl oz) cream, whipped
salt and freshly ground black pepper
cayenne pepper

1. Pour the wine into a saucepan and reduce over a high flame until it is about one-quarter of the original volume.
2. Steam the fish fillets for about 10 minutes, or until just cooked, but still very firm. Remove them and keep them warm.
3. Cut the hard butter into small pieces and, using a wire whisk, whip it into the reduced wine over a high heat. The butter should stay creamy.
4. Just before it reaches the boil whisk in the whipped cream.
5. Season with salt and freshly ground black pepper.
6. Serve the fish fillets with this sauce poured over the top, sprinkled with a little cayenne pepper.

Choux aux Lardons

Braised cabbage with bacon pieces
This can be served as a separate vegetable course or with meat, especially sausage or smoked meat.

Serves 6-8

1 tablespoon oil
30 g (1 oz) butter
1 large onion, thinly sliced
250 g (8 oz) bacon, cut into cubes

½ cabbage, chopped
1 clove garlic, crushed
salt and pepper
3 tablespoons dry white wine

1. In a heavy saucepan, heat the oil and butter.
2. Gently fry the onion without letting it colour.
3. Add the bacon cubes and cook gently for 5 minutes.
4. Add the cabbage and stir well, allowing it to fry gently without catching.
5. Add the garlic, salt and pepper and continue to cook, stirring all the time.
6. Add the wine and simmer gently until the cabbage is tender, but still crisp.
7. Serve immediately.

Capucin Gourmand, Nancy.
In France there seems to be a very fine line between a one-star and a two-star restaurant. Capucin Gourmand with its one star justifiably enjoys the reputation of being the top restaurant in Nancy. The food there was equal to, or better than, many higher rating restaurants. Even the humble Quiche Lorraine, when prepared by Gérard Veissière (right) appears as a gourmet creation. The selection of cheese offered by Madame Veissière, who looks after the dining room, was the most remarkable I encountered.

Above: *Chilled Raspberry Soufflé (p. 20).*

Oie à l'Alsacienne

Roast goose served with braised sauerkraut

Serves 6-8

1 goose 4-5 kg, (8-10 lb) ready for
  the oven
flour
1 tablespoon of butter, cut into pieces

Stuffing:
250 g (8 oz) sausage meat
2 tablespoons finely chopped parsley
1 tablespoon chopped fresh thyme

Braised Sauerkraut:
1 onion, finely chopped
250 g (8 oz) bacon and ham, chopped
  and mixed
750 g (1½ lb) sauerkraut
salt and freshly ground black pepper
500 g (1 lb) Strasbourg sausage
  (optional)

1. Preheat the oven to 210°C (425°F).
2. Mix the sausage meat with the parsley and thyme.
3. Sprinkle the back of the goose with a little flour, and the pieces of butter.
4. Stuff the goose with the stuffing mixture.
5. Roast the goose for 15 minutes, then reduce the oven temperature to 180°C (350°F) and continue roasting until the goose is tender (about 25 minutes per 500 g).
6. From time to time drain off and reserve some of the fat.
7. Using 2 tablespoons of goose fat in a heavy pan, cook the onion until it is soft and transparent.
8. Add the bacon and ham and continue to cook gently.
9. Drain the sauerkraut and rinse it well in fresh water. Drain it again.
10. Place the washed sauerkraut on top of the onions, bacon and ham and mix all the ingredients together, seasoning well.
11. Moisten with 1 cup of water, cover the pan and leave to cook very gently for 1 hour.
12. 10 minutes before serving, add the Strasbourg sausages to the sauerkraut.
13. Serve the goose on a bed of braised sauerkraut, with the diluted pan juices poured over the top.

Aiguillette de Caneton Sainte Alliance

Strips of duckling truffles, mushrooms and duck liver combined in a demi-glace sauce and covered with puff pastry
A recipe from Restaurant Capucin Gourmand in Nancy.

Serves 4

1 fat duckling, weighing 1.8-2 kg
  (3½-4 lb)
truffles (optional)
500 g (1 lb) mushrooms, sliced
1 duck's liver
½ recipe of demi-glace sauce made
  with duck carcase (see p. 149)

1 tablespoon cream
1 teaspoon white port
salt and freshly ground black pepper
½ recipe puff pastry (see p. 150)
1 egg yolk

1. Preheat the oven to 180°C (350°F).
2. Prick the skin of the duckling and bake for about 1 hour, allowing ¼ hour per 500 g.
3. Carve the meat from the bone, (it should be quite pink) and cut into julienne strips.
4. Use the duck carcase in preparing the demi-glace sauce.
5. Turn up the oven to 220°C (425°F).
6. Cut the truffles, mushrooms and duck's liver into strips, and combine with the duck meat.
7. Add two generous tablespoons of demi-glace sauce to this mixture.
8. Add the cream and port, and season with salt and pepper.
9. Transfer this mixture to an earthenware cocotte.
10. Cover with puff pastry, and brush the top with beaten egg yolk. Leave a small hole to allow the steam to escape.
11. Place in the oven for approximately 15 minutes, or until the pastry is cooked and golden brown.
12. Wrap the cocotte in a napkin and serve.

Poitrine de Veau Farcie

Stuffed breast of veal

Serves 6-8

1.5-2 kg (3-4 lb) breast of veal in
  one piece
lemon juice
salt and freshly ground black pepper
30 g (1 oz) + 2 tablespoons butter
1 onion, finely chopped

250 g (8 oz) spinach, chopped
250 g (8 oz) sausage meat
1 tablespoon finely chopped parsley
1 egg, beaten
flour
2 tablespoons oil

1. Preheat the oven to 160°C (325°F).
2. Wipe the veal on both sides with a damp cloth, sprinkle with lemon juice and season to taste with salt and freshly ground black pepper.
3. Melt 30 g of butter in a heavy saucepan and sauté the onion until it is transparent.
4. Add the spinach and cook until it is soft. Drain.
5. In a mixing bowl combine the sausage meat, parsley, beaten egg, onion and spinach mixture, salt and freshly ground pepper to taste.
6. Lay this mixture in the centre of the veal.
7. Roll the veal neatly, and sew up with fine string.
8. Dust the veal roll with flour.
9. Place it in a deep roasting pan with the remaining 2 tablespoons of butter and the oil.
10. Roast the veal for between 1½-2 hours, basting frequently. A little water may be added to the pan if necessary to keep it from drying out.
11. Slice the veal and serve immediately.

Côtes de Porc à la Vosgienne

Pork chops à la Vosgienne cooked with onions and mirabelle plums

Serves 6

1 tablespoon lard
6 pork loin chops
3 medium onions, chopped
500 g (1 lb) mirabelle plums
  (yellow plums), stoned

1 tablespoon white wine vinegar
½ cup (4 fl oz) dry white wine
½ cup (4 fl oz) concentrated veal stock
salt and freshly ground black pepper

1. Melt the lard in a large, heavy bottomed frying pan, and sauté the chops, turning so that they become golden on both sides.
2. When the chops are three-quarters cooked, add the onions to the pan and continue cooking gently.
3. Stone the plums and cook them over a very gentle heat with 3 tablespoons of water and no sugar for about 10 minutes.
4. Place the plums in the centre of a warmed serving dish and arrange the pork chops around them.
5. Skim as much fat off the juices in the pan as possible.
6. Pour the vinegar, white wine and veal stock into the pan and reduce over a vigorous heat.
7. Adjust the seasoning to taste.
8. Pour over the chops and serve.

Les Spätzle Alsacians

Alsacian dumplings
From the Hostellerie la Cheneaudiere in Colroy-la-Roche

2½ cups (10 oz) flour
3 eggs
2 cups (16 fl oz) milk (or water)
½ teaspoon salt

¼ teaspoon pepper
⅛ teaspoon nutmeg
90 g (3 oz) butter, melted

1. Place the flour in a bowl, whip the eggs lightly and while mixing with a wooden spoon, gradually incorporate them, together with the milk, salt, pepper and nutmeg into the flour. The texture of the dough should be smooth and almost flowing.
2. Spätzle are made with a special 'spätzle mill', however, if it is not available, the dough may be pressed through a colander into a saucepan of lightly boiling salted water.
3. The spätzle are cooked as soon as they rise to the surface. Place them in a colander and briefly rinse them under running water.
4. Before serving, heat the spaetzle in a saucepan with the melted butter.

Sauerkraut à la Strasbourgeoise

Sauerkraut Strasbourg style

Serves 8

pork fat, thinly sliced
2 large onions, sliced
2 cooking apples, cored and sliced
2 cloves garlic, coarsely chopped
2 kg (4 lb) sauerkraut, well washed
375 g (12 oz) salt pork
freshly ground black pepper

8 juniper berries, crushed
dry white wine to cover
1 boned loin of fresh or smoked pork
1 large garlic sausage
8-16 sausages (bratwurst, knockwurst, frankfurters or Strasbourgers)

1. Preheat the oven to 120°C (250°F).
2. Line a deep earthenware casserole or stockpot with thinly sliced pork fat.
3. Add half the onions, apples and garlic.
4. Place a thick layer of drained sauerkraut on top with a piece of salt pork.
5. Grind plenty of black pepper over the top.
6. Add the remaining onions, apples and garlic and the crushed juniper berries.
7. Cover with the remaining sauerkraut and add just enough dry white wine to cover the sauerkraut.
8. Cover and place in the oven for 4-6 hours; the longer it cooks, the better.
9. About 2½ hours before serving, add the loin of pork to the casserole dish, cover and continue to cook.
10. About 2 hours before serving, add the large garlic sausage and the selection of small sausages.
11. To serve, heap the sauerkraut in the middle of a large serving dish.
12. Slice the different meats and sausages and arrange around the sauerkraut. Boiled potatoes may be served as an accompaniment.

Hostellerie la Cheneaudière, Colroy-La-Roche.
La Cheneaudière is a hotel and restaurant situated in an out-of-the-way tranquil forest setting. It has the best food I have had in a restaurant that does not bear a Michelin Guide star. Monsieur and Madame François welcome their guests, while in the kitchen their son-in-law prepares delicious food based on ancient local recipes. It's 62 km from Strasbourg but well worth the journey.

Above: *A selection of dishes from the Hostellerie la Cheneaudière. Clockwise from bottom left: Saddle of Venison, Spätzles (p. 18), Sauté of Lobsters with Foie Gras.*

Soufflé Glacé aux Framboises Fraîches

Chilled fresh raspberry soufflé
A recipe from Restaurant Capucin Gourmand in Nancy.

Serves 4

500 g (1 lb) raspberries
1¼ cups (10 fl oz) cream, whipped
½ cup (4 oz) caster (powdered) sugar

1. Set a few raspberries aside for decoration, and crush the rest.
2. Add the whipped cream and the sugar, and mix together.
3. Take a soufflé dish and make a collar with greaseproof paper.
4. Pour in the soufflé mixture, and place in the coldest part of the refrigerator.
5. When ready to serve, remove the soufflé from the refrigerator and remove the paper collar.
6. Decorate the top with the remaining raspberries and a little icing sugar and serve.

Kugelhupf

Alsatian yeast cake
This very distinctive cake from Alsace is often eaten as an accompaniment to coffee. It is traditionally cooked in a special mould, but a large ring mould could be used instead.

Serves 8-10

½ cup (3 oz) raisins
3 tablespoons Kirsch (optional)
30 g (1 oz) fresh yeast
1 cup (8 fl oz) warm milk
⅓ cup (3 oz) sugar
500 g (1 lb) flour

½ teaspoon salt
2 eggs, beaten
200 g (7 oz) butter, softened
60 g (2 oz) almonds, chopped
icing (confectioners) sugar for dusting

1. Soak the raisins in the Kirsch, if used. If not, cover the raisins with tepid water and leave for 20 minutes. Drain.
2. Blend the yeast with half of the warm milk, 1 teaspoon of sugar and just enough of the flour to give a consistency of thin cream.
3. Leave in a warm place for 20 minutes until frothy.
4. Sift the remaining flour into a bowl.
5. Add the salt.
6. Stir in the remaining sugar.
7. Beat in the eggs and the rest of the milk.
8. Knead in the softened butter, and work the dough until it comes cleanly away from the sides of the bowl.
9. Add the yeast mixture and beat for a few minutes.
10. Cover with a damp cloth and leave in a warm place for 1 hour until well risen.
11. Knead the dough on a lightly floured board and incorporate the raisins.
12. Butter the kugelhupf mould or 30 cm (12 in) ring mould.
13. Scatter the almonds in the mould.
14. Press the dough into the mould. It should only half fill it.
15. Cover with a damp cloth again and leave in a warm place for 2 hours or until the dough has risen almost to the top of the tin.
16. Preheat the oven to 160°C (325°F).
17. Bake for 45 minutes. If the top appears to be browning too quickly, cover it with foil.
18. Leave the kugelhupf in the mould for at least 30 minutes before turning out.
19. Dust liberally with sifted icing sugar when cool.
20. Serve with coffee or tea within a day or two of baking. Kugelhupf is as its best when eaten fresh.

Tarte Alsacienne
Apple tart from Alsace

Serves 6

250 g (8 oz) short pastry (see p. 150)
4 large cooking apples, peeled, cored
  and thinly sliced
4 tablespoons sugar

2 eggs
1 tablespoon flour
½ cup (4 fl oz) milk or cream
Kirsch or brandy

1. Preheat the oven to 210°C (425°F).
2. Prepare the pastry. Roll out the pastry and line a 23 cm (9 in) tart tin.
3. Arrange the slices of apple on the pastry in circles.
4. Sprinkle with 1 tablespoon of the sugar.
5. Bake for 10 minutes.
6. In a mixing bowl, whisk the eggs.
7. Mix in the flour.
8. Add the milk or cream, whisking all the time, and then the remaining sugar.
9. Sprinkle into this mixture a little Kirsch or brandy.
10. Pour on to the hot partly-cooked tart.
11. Bake the tart for a further 20 minutes in the hot oven, until the top is cooked and the pastry golden brown. (This tart can also be made with stoned plums or cherries.)

Les Madeleines de Commercy
Commercy madeleines
These are delicate little cakes, baked in shell-shaped madeleine moulds. Makes approximately 30 madeleines.

¾ cup (6 oz) caster (powdered) sugar
1¼ cups (5 oz) flour, sieved
3 eggs
½ teaspoon bicarbonate of soda
  (baking soda)

grated rind of ½ a lemon
pinch of salt
75 g (2½ oz) butter, melted

1. Preheat the oven to 160°C (325°F).
2. Mix the sugar, flour, eggs, bicarbonate of soda, lemon rind and salt in a bowl, until the mixture is very smooth. This may be done in a food processor or electric mixer.
3. Add the melted butter and mix well.
4. Butter a tray of special madeleine moulds, or indented baking tray.
5. Fill the moulds two thirds full of the mixture.
6. Bake in the preheated oven, for 15-20 minutes.
7. Turn on to a wire rack to cool.

Burgundy

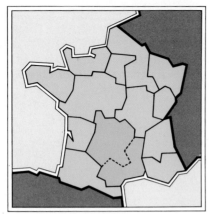

No other region in France combines great wines and great food in such a harmonious way as in Burgundy.

In the north, Lower Burgundy, of which Auxerre is the main town, produces Chablis, a fine light wine which accounts for that area's light, subtle cuisine. It is the perfect complement to pike, trout, salmon trout and crayfish which abound in the many rivers of the region.

In Central Burgundy, where the capital, Dijon, is situated, we find, south of the city, the full bodied wines of the Côte d'Or, The Golden Slope. The place names are wine legend: Gevrey-Chambertin, Vosne-Romanée, Nuits-Saint-Georges, Beaune, Volnay, Meursault. The food the region produces is hearty and the most typical of the Burgundy cuisine: Boeuf à la Bourguignonne, Escargots à la Bourguignonne and of course Coq au Vin, to name the most famous dishes.

Further south, the Charolles district produces the best beef in France and the chickens of Bresse have no equal.

While not part of Burgundy proper, the Lyonnais and Lyon, its capital, form part of that gastronomic region and are a sparkling jewel in its crown. Considered as the culinary capital of France, the food of Lyon is strongly influenced by Beaujolais, the wine from Burgundy's southern vineyards. No wonder then, that with all the elements in its favour, Lyon and its surroundings, have attracted some of the greatest chefs of France. Only second to Paris, the area boasts many Michelin Guide two and three star restaurants.

The food throughout the region is full-bodied and hearty like most of its wines. It is, as has been said, 'cuisine bourgeoise at its best'.

But the fame of Burgundy does not rest entirely on its wines and food.

Throughout the ages it has played an important historical and cultural part.

Today a journey through that region is very rewarding. There is no better place to start than Dijon, its capital. Many buildings there bear witness to a great past. The former Ducal Palace is of particular interest to the gourmet traveller as it incorporates the mediaeval kitchen with its gigantic fireplaces where great feasts were prepared in the past. The ruins of many famous abbeys and castles can be found in the countryside. Regretfully few have survived the ravages of time and wars.

Cluny, once the chief monastery of the Benedictines, after whom the famous liqueur is named and Citeaux, the abbey of the strict Cistercian monks are today just ruins.

But it was in some of these monasteries and at the Ducal Court, that the excellent food that Burgundy offers today was created.

Vineyard in Burgundy

Escargots à la Bourguignonne

Snails in Burgundy sauce
The snails from this region are fed on grape leaves, and are much prized by connoisseurs,
who claim them to be the best in France.

Serves 4

4 dozen snails (if tinned snails are
being used, only the ingredients for
Burgundy Butter are needed)
1 cup (7 oz) rock salt
1 cup (8 fl oz) wine vinegar
½ cup (2 oz) flour

Stock:
1 bottle white Burgundy
3 cups (24 fl oz) chicken stock
2 carrots, finely chopped
2 onions, finely chopped

bouquet garni
generous pinch of thyme
salt and white pepper

Burgundy Butter:
375 g (12 oz) butter
2 tablespoons finely chopped parsley
3 cloves garlic, crushed
1 tablespoon very finely chopped
spring onions (scallions)
1 tablespoon salt
freshly ground black pepper to taste

1. Remove the hard covering which seals the snail in the shell.
2. Wash the snails thoroughly under running water.
3. Leave them for 2 hours in a good amount of water with the rock salt, vinegar and flour.
4. Wash the snails again.
5. Blanch them in a large saucepan of boiling water for 5 minutes.
6. Drain them and run them under cold water.
7. Take each snail out of its shell and cut off the black part at the end of its body.
8. Put the snails in a large, clean saucepan with the white wine and the stock. (The liquid should completely cover the snails.)
9. Add the carrots, onions, bouquet garni, thyme, salt and pepper and simmer over a very low heat for about 4 hours.
10. Leave the snails to cool in the liquid. Drain.
11. Preheat the oven to 160°C (325°F).
12. To prepare the Burgundy butter, combine the butter, parsley, garlic, spring onions, salt and pepper, and work together with a fork to obtain a smooth paste.
13. Press a nut of butter into each shell. Add a well drained snail to each shell and another nut of the butter, smoothing off with the flat of a knife, so that the butter is level with the shell.
14. Arrange the snails on special snail dishes, or any ovenproof serving dish.
15. Heat for a few minutes in the oven, without letting the butter boil.
16. Serve immediately with very fresh French bread which is used to soak up the butter that escapes from the snails.

Pommes Lyonnaises

Potatoes sautéed with onions

Serves 6

1 kg (2 lb) potatoes
155 g (5 oz) butter
4 onions, finely sliced

salt and pepper
finely chopped parsley

1. Peel and slice the potatoes thinly and dry them well.
2. Melt 90 g of the butter in a heavy bottomed frying pan.
3. Fry the potatoes in the butter over a medium heat, turning them regularly until they are a golden brown colour and evenly cooked.
4. In a separate pan, melt the remaining butter and gently fry the onions, until they are a golden brown colour.
5. Add the onions to the potatoes and continue cooking, shaking the pan so that the potatoes and onions are well mixed.
6. When they are both cooked, season with salt and freshly ground black pepper.
7. Serve in a vegetable dish, sprinkled with chopped parsley.

Omelette à la Lyonnaise

Omelette with onions and parsley

Serves 4

60 g (2 oz) butter	**1 tablespoon cold water**
4 onions, finely sliced	**salt and pepper**
8 eggs	**2 tablespoons finely chopped parsley**

1. Melt half the butter in a heavy frying pan, and gently sauté the onions until they are soft and golden in colour. Allow to cool a little.
2. In a mixing bowl, beat the eggs together with the water, salt and pepper.
3. Add the cooked onions and parsley.
4. Melt a knob of butter in the omelette pan and pour in the egg mixture.
5. Proceed to cook the omelette in the normal way.
6. When the omelette is cooked, fold it over and slide it on to a warmed serving dish.
7. Melt the remaining butter in the pan, and when it turns a golden colour, pour it over the omelette and serve.

Flamiche aux Poireaux

Leek tart

Serves 6

500 g (1 lb) leeks, cleaned	**salt and freshly ground black pepper**
90 g (3 oz) butter	**500 g (1 lb) puff pastry (see p. 150)**
3-4 tablespoons water	**1 egg yolk, mixed with a little water**
4 tablespoons thick cream	

1. Preheat the oven to 200°C (400°F).
2. Chop the leeks finely, using all the white part and very little of the green.
3. Melt half the butter in a heavy pan and stew the leeks gently, gradually adding the rest of the butter as they are cooking.
4. Moisten with the water, cover and cook gently until the leeks are quite soft and all the liquid has been absorbed.
5. Add the cream and season well.
6. Prepare the pastry and divide it into two.
7. Roll out half into a thin round and place it on a damp baking sheet.
8. Place the leek mixture in the middle, leaving a border of 3 cm (1½ in) all round.
9. Brush the border with water.
10. Roll out the rest of the pastry in the same way and place on top of the leek mixture.
11. Press the edges firmly together so that they are well sealed.
12. To help the pastry to rise, feather the edges with a sharp knife.
13. Glaze the surface by brushing with diluted egg yolk, and make a trellis pattern with the point of a knife.
14. Cook the tart for 10 minutes.
15. Reduce the heat to 180°C (350°F) and cook for a further 20-25 minutes until the surface of the pastry is golden.
16. The tart should be served very hot, but it may be cooked in advance and reheated.

Salade de Queues d'Écrevisses

Freshwater Crayfish Salad
This recipe comes from the Restaurant Nandron in Lyon. King prawns may also be used
for this dish.

Serves 4

1.5 kg (3 lb) crayfish (yabbies) or
  king prawns
6 cups (1.5 litres) fish stock
500 g (1 lb) string beans
4 artichoke hearts
1 tomato, peeled and cut into quarters

2 hard-boiled eggs, cut into quarters
6 cos lettuce leaves
½ cup (4 fl oz) cream, whipped
1 teaspoon finely chopped
  fresh tarragon
1 cup (8 fl oz) mayonnaise

1. Boil the crayfish or king prawns in the fish stock for 3 minutes.
2. Remove them from the stock and peel the tails.
3. Top and tail the beans and without cutting them steam or boil them until they are cooked but still firm (not more than 5 minutes).
4. If using fresh artichokes, boil them for 15 minutes in salted water. When cooked remove the leaves and the choke, using only the artichoke bottom.
5. To assemble the salad, arrange the tails, beans, artichoke hearts, tomatoes, hard-boiled eggs and lettuce leaves on a serving dish. Mix the whipped cream and tarragon leaves into the mayonnaise and spoon it over the salad.

Quenelles of Pike 'Gérard Nandron'

From the Restaurant Nandron in Lyon. There are several recipes for pike in this book but
as Gérard Nandron's quenelles were exceptionally good when I tasted them I include his
own method as it differs from the others. Snapper, gemfish or jewfish may be used instead
of pike, however, the result may not be quite as good.

Serves 6

1 kg (2 lb) fish fillets, chilled
4 cups (1 litre) fresh cream
½ teaspoon salt
cayenne pepper

125 g (4 oz) melted clarified butter
3 whole eggs
1½ cups (12 fl oz) Mornay Sauce

1. In a food processor, process the fish until very fine. If you haven't got a food processor, rub the finely chopped flesh through a sieve.
2. Place it into a bowl set over ice and slowly incorporate the cream, beating it firmly with a wooden spoon. If an electric mixer is available, this can be done using a paddle attachment. The resulting mixture should have the consistency of a heavy mayonnaise.
3. Add the salt and pepper and slowly incorporate the butter and the eggs.
4. Refrigerate the mixture for 24 hours.
5. Form the quenelles, one large or two smaller ones per person, by rolling them into shape on a floured board.
6. Gently poach them in simmering salted water for about 5 minutes.
7. To serve, pour some of the Mornay Sauce over each quenelle. Place them under a grill and serve when the sauce browns a little.

Restaurant Nandron, Lyon.

Gérard Nandron, at his restaurant in Quai Jean Mulin along the banks of the Rhône, prepares some of the best food in the city, a great credit to him, as Lyon, by reputation, is the gastronomic capital of France and has attracted some of the greatest chefs in the country. His Quenelle de Brochet 'Gérard Nandron' is light and full of flavour, while the sweetbreads with truffles enjoy a well-deserved reputation. In the dining room, decorated in the style of the 1930s, his charming wife with a team of attentive waiters helps to make a meal at Nandron a memorable occasion.

Above and right: *Light and delicate Quenelles of Pike as served by Gérard Nandron at his restaurant in Lyon.*

Queues d'Écrevisses à la Nantua

Freshwater crayfish tails with Nantua sauce

Serves 6

Mirepoix:
30 g (1 oz) butter
2 carrots, finely chopped
2 onions, finely chopped
1 stick celery, finely chopped
sprig of thyme
bay leaf
48 raw crayfish tails, or large prawns

salt and freshly ground black pepper
1 cup (8 fl oz) dry white wine
½ cup (4 fl oz) Béchamel sauce
  (see p. 147)
90 g (3 oz) butter
¼ cup (1 oz) flour
2 tablespoons brandy
½ cup (4 fl oz) cream

1. To make the mirepoix, melt the 30 g of butter in a heavy pan, and gently cook the carrots, onions, celery, thyme and bay leaf until very tender.
2. Add the crayfish tails or prawns to the mirepoix.
3. Season with salt and pepper.
4. Moisten with the wine.
5. Cover the pan and simmer gently for 10 minutes.
6. Drain the crayfish and shell them, reserving the shells, the mirepoix and the liquid.
7. Pound the shells and the mirepoix in a mortar or food processor.
8. Prepare the Béchamel sauce.
9. Strain the shell-and-mirepoix purée and add to the Béchamel sauce with the reserved liquid whisking well. This is the sauce Nantua.
10. Put the crayfish tails in a small pan with 30 g of butter.
11. Sprinkle with the flour.
12. Mix thoroughly.
13. Add the brandy and cream.
14. Simmer on a low heat for 8 minutes.
15. Add the sauce Nantua to the pan and heat through.
16. Remove the pan from the heat and whisk in the remaining 60 g of butter.
17. Serve immediately.

Poularde Pochée Demi-Deuil

Poached chicken in half-mourning

Serves 6

60 g (2 oz) truffles, finely sliced
2 chickens, each weighing about
  1.2 kg (2¼ lb)
6 leeks, white part only
8 small carrots, scraped

2 turnips, peeled
2 stalks celery
60 g (2 oz) bacon, diced
185 g (6 oz) butter
salt and freshly ground black pepper

1. Insert the slices of truffles under the breast skin of the chickens and truss the birds.
2. Put the leeks, carrots, turnips, celery and bacon into a large casserole.
3. Add about 8 cups (2 litres) of water.
4. Add salt and pepper to taste, and simmer gently for 1 hour.
5. Add the chickens to the casserole, making sure that there is enough liquid to cover them.
6. Cover the casserole and simmer gently for 25 minutes.
7. Remove the vegetables from the stock, but leave the chickens in the casserole covered, with the heat turned off but still on the stove, for another 20 minutes.
8. In a heavy frying pan melt 125 g of the butter.
9. Gently stew the vegetables in the butter. They are served as an accompaniment to the chicken.
10. Drain the chickens and arrange them on a serving dish and keep warm.
11. Remove the fat from the stock, pour about 4 cups of it into a small heavy saucepan, and boil over a high heat until it is reduced by half.
12. Whisk in the remaining butter until the sauce is light and fluffy.
13. Pour the sauce over the chickens and serve.

Pauchouse

A matelote of mixed fish in white wine and cream sauce
In Burgundy only freshwater fish are used to make Pauchouse, but a similar dish could be made from a mixture of fish from the sea.

Serves 6-8

2 kg (4 lb) mixed fish
2 carrots, chopped
2 onions, chopped
salt and pepper
bouquet garni
2 cups (16 fl oz) white wine
90 g (3 oz) butter

½ cup (2 oz) flour
½ cup (4 fl oz) cream
125 g (4 oz) streaky (fat) bacon, chopped
90 g (3 oz) mushrooms, chopped
parsley
croûtons

1. Clean the fish and cut off the heads.
2. Oil a large pot, and line it with the chopped carrots and onions.
3. Add salt, freshly ground black pepper and the bouquet garni.
4. Cut the fish into chunks and arrange them on the vegetables.
5. Cover with the white wine, or a mixture of white wine and water.
6. Simmer gently for about 20 minutes, or until the fish is just cooked.
7. Drain the fish and place it in a deep serving dish.
8. Strain the stock through a fine sieve and return it to the pan.
9. Mix 60 g of the butter with the flour to make a beurre manié.
10. Stir this butter mixture into the stock while heating, whisking all the time so that the sauce thickens smoothly.
11. Add the cream and correct the seasoning.
12. Pour this hot sauce over the fish and keep warm.
13. Toss the chopped bacon and mushrooms in the remaining butter.
14. Sprinkle these over the top of the fish and decorate with parsley.
15. Serve with croûtons.

Jambon à la Crème de Saulieu

Ham in rich cream sauce

Serves 6

300 g (10 oz) button mushrooms, thinly sliced
30 g (1 oz) + 1 tablespoon butter
salt and freshly ground black pepper
¾ cup (6 fl oz) dry white wine
3 tablespoons finely chopped spring onions (scallions)

2 cups (16 fl oz) cream
300 g (10 oz) tomatoes, peeled, seeded and chopped
1 tablespoon flour
18 fairly thick slices of cooked ham (about 60 g (2 oz) each)
½ cup (2 oz) grated Parmesan cheese

1. Cook the mushrooms in 30 g of the butter for about 3 minutes, until they are softened and slightly cooked.
2. Season them with salt and freshly ground black pepper.
3. Remove the mushrooms from the pan and reserve.
4. Add the wine and the spring onions to the pan and reduce to half the original quantity.
5. Add the cream, tomatoes and seasoning and boil gently for 5 to 6 minutes.
6. Combine the remaining butter with the flour to make a beurre manié.
7. Stirring well all the time, blend the beurre manié into the sauce.
8. Arrange the slices of ham in a lightly buttered deep metal dish.
9. Sprinkle the ham with the mushrooms and cover with the sauce.
10. Sprinkle the top with the Parmesan cheese.
11. Glaze quickly under the grill, making sure that the sauce does not boil and serve.

Les Oeufs en Meurette

Eggs in red wine sauce
This recipe comes from La Rôtisserie du Chambertin in Gevrey-Chambertin.

Serves 4

4 eggs
vinegar water

Sauce Bourguignonne:
3 spring onions (scallions), chopped
3 tablespoons mixed fresh herbs
2 cups (16 fl oz) dry red wine
2 cups (16 fl oz) beef, veal or
  chicken stock

2 tablespoons kneaded butter made
  with one tablespoon of softened
  butter and 1 tablespoon of flour
50 g (1¾ oz) butter
salt
freshly ground pepper

1. Poach the eggs in the vinegar water and place them on a heated plate.
2. To serve, mask with the sauce.
3. The eggs may also be served with sautéed button mushrooms and glazed small onions.

Sauce Bourguignonne:
1. Add the onions and the herbs to the wine and stock. Boil to reduce by half.
2. Add the kneaded butter and gently cook for a few minutes.
3. In the last moment finish off with the butter and season.

Le Coq au Vin du Pays

From La Rôtisserie du Chambertin in Gevrey-Chambertin.

Serves 4

1.5 kg (3 lb) chicken
30 g (1 oz) butter
½ cup (4 fl oz) Marc de Bourgogne
  or brandy
giblets
½ cup (2 oz) flour
salt
freshly ground black pepper

Marinade:
2 onions, roughly chopped
2 carrots, sliced
2 stalks celery, cut in 1.25 cm
  (½ in) lengths
2 spring onions (scallions),
  roughly chopped
1 clove garlic, chopped
2 sprigs thyme, chopped
2 bay leaves
4 sprigs parsley, chopped
2 cloves
3 cups (24 fl oz) dry, Burgundy-style
  red wine
½ cup (4 fl oz) wine vinegar
¼ cup (2 fl oz) olive oil

1. Cut the chicken into pieces, place them into a large container and add all the marinade ingredients. Marinate overnight.
2. Take out the chicken pieces and brown them lightly in the butter.
3. Add the Marc or brandy and flame.
4. Transfer the chicken pieces, the marinade, including all its ingredients, and the giblets into a flameproof casserole dish.
5. Cover and simmer for approximately 1½ hours, checking the chicken to see if it is tender.
6. Strain the cooking liquid into a saucepan and add the chicken pieces.
7. Mix the flour with some water and pour it into the cooking liquid.
8. Slowly boil the liquid, stirring constantly until it thickens.
9. Season and serve with sautéed button mushrooms and small onions.

La Rôtisserie du Chambertin, Gevrey-Chambertin.

12 km south of Dijon the vineyards of Gevrey-Chambertin produce some of the finest Burgundy wine, complementing the outstanding local food. In the village, I found 'La Rôtisserie du Chambertin', an unusual restaurant run by Céline and Pierre Menneveau. It is unusual in that, among the top restaurants in France, it is not customary to find a woman presiding over the kitchen. While Pierre Menneveau is the gracious host, Céline (right) produces fine examples of classical and regional cuisine. There is no better place to try traditional Escargots des Champs or 'true' Coq au Vin.

Above: *Coq au Vin, the most famous dish in Burgundy, cooked in the traditional way by Madame Menneveau.*

Boeuf à la Bourguignonne

Burgundy beef
This is one of the great dishes of French cuisine, which, like many wine-based dishes, is better when reheated and served on the following day.

Serves 6

1.5 kg (3 lb) topside of beef
flour
4 tablespoons oil
90 g (3 oz) + 1 tablespoon butter
125 g (4 oz) salt pork, diced
salt and freshly ground black pepper
4 tablespoons brandy, warmed
2 carrots, chopped
1 leek, chopped
4 spring onions (scallions), chopped
1 large onion, chopped

1 clove garlic, crushed
1 calf's foot (optional)
bouquet garni
½ bottle Burgundy
beef stock to cover
1 tablespoon flour
18 pickling onions
18 button mushrooms
sugar
lemon juice
chopped parsley

1. Preheat oven to 150°C (300°F).
2. Cut the beef into cubes, roll them in flour.
3. Heat 2 tablespoons of oil with 2 tablespoons of butter, in a large heavy frying pan.
4. Sauté the salt pork until crisp and brown.
5. Remove the pork from the pan and transfer to a large earthenware casserole.
6. Brown the beef well on all sides in the fat remaining in the pan and season with salt and freshly ground pepper.
7. Pour the warmed brandy over the meat and ignite.
8. Let the flame burn away and add the meat to the casserole.
9. Cook the carrots, leek, spring onions, onion and garlic in the remaining fat in the frying pan, stirring until they are browned.
10. Transfer the vegetables to the casserole dish with the meat.
11. Add the calf's foot and the bouquet garni to the casserole.
12. Pour over all but 4 tablespoons of the wine, and just enough beef stock to cover the contents of the casserole.
13. Cover and cook in a very slow oven (150°C reducing to 120°C) for two hours. The secret of a good boeuf bourgignonne is very slow, gentle cooking.
14. Remove the fat from the sauce.
15. On a saucer, work together 1 tablespoon of flour with 1 tablespoon of soft butter to make a beurre manié.
16. Stir this butter and flour mixture into the casserole.
17. Cover and cook very gently for a further 2 hours.
18. Brown the small onions in 1 tablespoon butter in a saucepan with a pinch of sugar.
19. Add the remaining 4 tablespoons of red wine, cover and cook very gently until the onions are almost tender. Keep warm.
20. Sauté the mushrooms in the remaining oil and butter and a little lemon juice. Keep warm.
21. When the meat is tender, remove the calf's foot and bouquet garni.
22. Correct the seasoning, add the onions and mushrooms.
23. Sprinkle with chopped parsley and serve.

Rumsteck Amoureuse à la Dijonnaise
Rump steak with mustard and cream sauce

Serves 2

1 piece of rump steak, weighing about
   500 g (1 lb)
salt and crushed black peppercorns
1 tablespoon oil
1 tablespoon butter
2 tablespoons brandy, warmed

Sauce:
3 tablespoons dry white wine
1 tablespoon butter
½ clove garlic, crushed
2 teaspoons fresh tarragon,
   finely chopped
1 tablespoon strong Dijon mustard
3 tablespoons thick cream
salt and freshly ground black pepper

1. Season the steak with salt and peppercorns, and brush it with a little oil.
2. Heat the butter and oil in a heavy pan, and when it is very hot put in the steak.
3. Cook the steak, turning only once, to the desired degree.
4. Remove the pan from the heat, pour the warmed brandy over it and ignite.
5. When the flames have died down, transfer the steak to a serving dish and keep it warm.
6. To make the sauce, deglaze the pan with the wine, add the butter and bring to the boil for a few seconds.
7. Pour this liquid into a small saucepan.
8. Add the garlic, tarragon and mustard to the saucepan, whisking well.
9. Add the cream, and heat over a very low heat, whisking all the time until the sauce is very hot but not boiling.
10. Check the seasoning, adding salt and freshly ground black pepper if necessary.
11. Pour the sauce over the meat and serve immediately.

Pognon
Burgundy griddle cakes

Serves 4-6

2 cups (8 oz) flour
¾ cup (6 oz) sugar
pinch of salt
60 g (2 oz) butter, soft

1¼ cups (10 fl oz) cream,
   whipped thick
yolk of 1 egg
1 tablespoon of milk

1. Preheat the oven to 210°C (425°F).
2. In a bowl, mix the flour, sugar and salt.
3. Rub in the butter.
4. Add the cream and mix well, forming a ball of dough.
5. Flour a board, and roll out to a round that is 1 cm (½ in) thick.
6. Transfer to an oiled baking sheet.
7. Brush with the yolk of egg, mixed with a little milk.
8. Decorate with incised lines.
9. Bake for 15 minutes.
10. Serve while still warm with butter or jam, or spread with cream cheese.

Franche-Comté, Savoy, Dauphiné

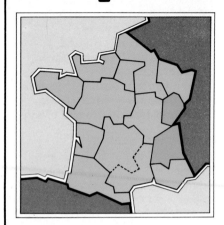

These three regions, while having their own characteristic cuisines, have a number of gastronomic elements in common. Their forests and meadows abound in fragrant herbs and grasses which accounts for some very tasty beef, and the rich milk from their cows produces some of the best cheese in the country. Swift, icy cold mountain streams yield trout and salmon trout and the rivers are rich in pike, the fish best suited for the regional speciality: the quenelle. The delicious freshwater crayfish appears on the table in Savoy as a gratin dish. The forests harbour feathered as well as furred game: Jugged Hare à la Franc-Comtoise, and the thrush pâtés des Alpes of the Savoy region are two examples of game cooking. The region produces good fresh vegetables and the fruit from the mountain orchards has fragrance and aroma.

The wines of the Franche-Comté have a special character and the yellow wine of Arbois is much appreciated. The Savoy and the Dauphiné produce some quality wines too, which regrettably are best known in their own region.

Franche-Comté, Savoy and the Dauphiné all have excellent skiing areas; those in the Savoy are probably the best in France. Skiers from all over the world flock to these provinces to enjoy the double delights of alpine skiing and excellent food. The summer here is just as popular as the winter. Walks in the Jura Mountains offer spectacular views.

Another famous tourist attraction is the Spa of Evian on the Lake of Geneva or, as it is known in French, Lac Leman. Other lakes combine natural beauty and gourmet pleasures. This is especially true of Lake Annecy where the Auberge du Père Bise, one of France's top three-star restaurants has been offering top quality food for more than three generations.

Wherever he goes in the this part of the country, the traveller will find a happy combination of exceptionally good food and some of the best scenery in France.

Restaurant du Père Bise on Lake Annecy in the Savoy.

Soupe de Grenouilles

Frogs' legs soup
Frogs' legs are one of the delicacies of this region which abounds with rivers, lakes and ponds.

Serves 4

3 cups (24 fl oz) fish fumet (see p. 149)
24 frogs' legs (these can be obtained
  frozen or tinned)
⅔ cup (5 fl oz) dry white wine
1 chopped spring onion (scallion)

1 sprig tarragon
salt and freshly ground black pepper
1 bunch watercress
2 egg yolks
2 tablespoons cream

1. Prepare the fish fumet, and bring to the boil in a large saucepan.
2. Drop in the frogs' legs and bring the liquid back to the boil.
3. When the liquid is boiling again, remove the frogs' legs, drain them well and keep them covered.
4. Put the white wine, spring onion, tarragon, salt and pepper into a small saucepan.
5. Bring these to the boil and reduce, uncovered, until the wine has all but evaporated.
6. Add it to the fumet in which the frogs' legs were poached.
7. Wash the watercress and remove and discard the larger stalks.
8. Add to the stock and simmer for 7 minutes, no longer or the watercress will lose its colour.
9. Purée the watercress and the stock in the blender.
10. Bone the frogs' legs. Keep warm.
11. Beat the egg yolks and the cream together.
12. Whisk this mixture into the purée, stirring constantly.
13. Heat through and check the seasoning, but do not allow it to boil.
14. Arrange the boned frogs' legs in soup bowls.
15. Cover them with the hot soup.
16. Decorate each bowl with a few watercress leaves, and serve.

Quenelles de Brochet Vesaul

Pike quenelles Vesaul style, in Financière sauce

Serves 4-6

1.85 kg (3¾ lb) boneless pike meat
  (any firm white fleshed fish may
  be substituted)
185 g (6 oz) butter
3 eggs
salt and freshly ground black pepper

Financière sauce:
2 cups (16 fl oz) Béchamel sauce
  (see p. 147)
125 g (4 oz) mushrooms,
  finely chopped
2 tablespoons lemon juice
½ cup (4 fl oz) Madeira

1. Pound the fish in a mortar, adding the butter bit by bit until it forms a smooth paste, or use a food mill, electric blender, or food processor.
2. Add the eggs, one by one.
3. Season to taste with salt and pepper.
4. Leave for 3 or 4 hours in a cool place, or in the refrigerator.
5. Preheat the oven to 210°C (425°F).
6. Form the mixture into small sausage-shaped quenelles.
7. Bring a large saucepan of salted water to the boil.
8. Poach the quenelles in the water for about 20 minutes.
9. Drain them well, and arrange on a flameproof serving dish.
10. Prepare the sauce by making 2 cups of Béchamel.
11. Place the chopped mushrooms into a small saucepan with the lemon juice and 1 tablespoon of water and cook for 5 minutes.
12. Add the drained mushrooms to the Béchamel sauce.
13. Add the Madeira to the sauce and cook a few minutes longer.
14. Cover the quenelles with the sauce.
15. Cook in the oven for about 15 minutes. The quenelles should treble in size.
16. Serve immediately.

Truite Amandine

Fried trout with almonds

Serves 4-6

4-6 trout
salt and freshly ground black pepper
milk
flour
125 g (4 oz) butter

1 tablespoon oil
4-6 tablespoons slivered almonds
juice of 1 lemon
3 tablespoons finely chopped parsley

1. Season the cleaned trout with salt and a little pepper.
2. Dip them in milk and then in flour.
3. Melt half the butter with the oil.
4. Sauté the fish until golden brown on both sides, about 5 minutes a side.
5. Remove the trout from the pan and keep them warm.
6. Drain the fat from the pan, and melt the remaining butter.
7. Add the blanched, slivered almonds and cook, shaking the pan continuously until the almonds are golden brown.
8. Add the lemon juice and parsley and pour over the trout.
9. Serve.

Anguille Savoyarde

Eel stuffed with puréed fish
If you can't buy eel, use any firm fleshed white fish.

Serves 6

Forcemeat:
1 cup (8 fl oz) milk
3 cups (6 oz) soft breadcrumbs
500 g (1 lb) boned skinned pike
  (or similar white fish)
salt and pepper
pinch of nutmeg
185 g (6 oz) butter, softened
2 whole eggs
4 egg yolks

1 eel or similar fish (have the
  fishmonger skin the fish and
  remove the backbone)
salt and pepper
250 g (8 oz) bacon slices
1 onion, chopped
1 carrot, chopped
125 g (4 oz) butter
bouquet garni
2 cups (16 fl oz) dry white wine
250 g (8 oz) button mushrooms
½ cup (2 oz) flour
1 cup (8 fl oz) cream

1. Prepare the forcemeat by soaking the breadcrumbs in the milk.
2. Blend the pike flesh, salt, pepper and nutmeg in an electric blender, then add the breadcrumbs.
3. Add the butter, the whole eggs and the egg yolks, blending well.
4. Lay the eel flat and season it with salt and pepper.
5. Spread the pike forcemeat on the inside.
6. Re-shape the eel and wrap it in slices of bacon, securing with toothpicks where necessary to ensure it keeps its shape.
7. Twist the eel into a ring shape.
8. In a large frying pan, fry the onion and carrot in 30 g of the butter.
9. Carefully place the eel on top of these vegetables.
10. Add a bouquet garni and pour in the wine, to almost cover the fish.
11. Bring to the boil and simmer gently without a lid for 30 minutes, removing any scum which may form.
12. In a separate pan, toss the mushrooms in 30 g of the butter.
13. Drain the eel and place it carefully into another dish, arranging the mushrooms around it.
14. In a clean saucepan, melt the remaining butter, add the flour and stir to make a roux.
15. Add the strained fish stock, blending well.
16. When the sauce has thickened, add the cream. Heat through, pour over the eel and serve.

Potée Franc-Comtoise

Like many of the regions of France, Franche-Comté has its own version of the Potée, characterised by the addition of Morteau sausage, although any variety of sausage intended for boiling may be substituted.

Serves 6

60 g (2 oz) butter
2 tablespoons oil
1 large onion, chopped
250 g (8 oz) pork belly, cut in pieces
500 g (1 lb) salt pork, cut in pieces
1 boiling sausage, cut in pieces
500 g (1 lb) carrots, sliced
1 kg (2 lb) potatoes, peeled and cut
  in pieces

2 cloves garlic, chopped
salt
freshly ground black pepper
bayleaf
thyme
1 large firm cabbage, cut in chunks
1 cup (8 fl oz) dry white wine

1. Preheat the oven to 180°C (350°F).
2. Melt the butter and oil in a large pot.
3. Add the chopped onion and cook until it is transparent.
4. Add the meat and the sausage.
5. Add the carrots, potatoes and garlic. Turn the ingredients and let them sizzle in the pan.
6. Add the salt, pepper and herbs, then the chunks of cabbage.
7. Pour in the white wine, and add a little water as well if necessary.
8. Cover tightly, and braise in the oven until the meat is tender, about 1½ hours.

Poireaux au Vin Blanc

Leeks in White Wine Sauce

Serves 6

6 leeks, white part only
50 g (1½ oz) butter
50 g (1½ oz) flour
1½-2 cups (12-16 fl oz) dry white
  wine, heated

½ cup (4 fl oz) cream
salt
freshly ground pepper
90 g (3 oz) Gruyère style cheese, grated

1. Preheat the oven to 190°C (375°F).
2. Cut the leeks into 10 cm (4 in) lengths and wash them thoroughly.
3. Boil the leeks in salted water for 15 minutes.
4. Pour off the water and arrange the leeks on the bottom of a buttered gratin dish.
5. In a saucepan make a white roux: melt the butter, add the flour and cook for a few minutes without browning it.
6. Add the hot wine and stir to avoid lumps. Cook for 5 minutes.
7. Add the cream and season.
8. Pour the sauce over the leeks and sprinkle with the cheese.
9. Cook in the oven for approximately 20 minutes. If necessary place under grill to brown the top.

Buisson d'Écrevisses Nage

Crayfish cooked in court-bouillon
From the Restaurant Auberge du Père Bise in Talloires.

Serves 6

5 cups (1.25 litres) water
4 cups (1 litre) dry white wine
2 carrots, finely chopped
3 spring onions (scallions)
   finely chopped
fresh thyme
bay leaf

1 stalk of celery, chopped
freshly ground pepper
3 small red peppers, finely chopped
a pinch of cayenne
salt
3 tablespoons brandy
24 live fresh water crayfish (yabbies)

1. In a large saucepan, combine the water, wine, carrots, spring onions, thyme, bay leaf, celery, pepper, red peppers, cayenne and salt and simmer gently for 20 minutes.
2. Add the brandy.
3. The court-bouillon is now ready for the crayfish.
4. Wash the crayfish and add them to the boiling court-bouillon.
5. Reduce the heat and simmer them for 5 minutes.
6. Remove them from the pan and serve hot with melted butter, lemon juice or mayonnaise.

La Mousse de Foies de Volailles

Chicken Liver Mousse
From the Restaurant Auberge du Père Bise in Talloires.

Serves 8

500 g (1 lb) chicken livers
500 g (1 lb) fresh belly of pork
½ cup (4 fl oz) dry Port wine
1 bay leaf
sprig of thyme
sprig of parsley

salt and freshly ground black pepper
250 g (8 oz) salt pork, blanched and
   cut into thin strips
500 g (1 lb) foie gras, tinned
⅓ cup (2½ fl oz) cream

1. Put the chicken livers and the pork into a bowl with the port, bay leaf, thyme, parsley, salt and pepper and marinate overnight.
2. Preheat the oven to 175°C (325°F).
3. Remove the bay leaf, thyme and parsley, and put the livers and pork through the fine blade of a food processor or mill.
4. Line a terrine with half the salt pork strips and fill the terrine with the liver mixture.
5. Cover with the remaining strips of salt pork and cover the terrine.
6. Put it in a baking tin half filled with water and cook for about 1½ hours in a slow oven at 175°C (325°F).
7. Cool and remove the fat surrounding it.
8. Mash the foie gras into the liver mixture and blend thoroughly in an electric blender.
9. Add the cream, mixing well.
10. Put into a mould and chill overnight in the refrigerator.
11. The liver mousse may be served with a port wine jelly.

La Poularde de Bresse Braisée à la Crème d'Estragon

*Chicken stuffed with fresh tarragon and served in a cream sauce flavoured with tarragon
Corn is cultivated intensively around Bresse, to be fed to the famous poultry of the region,
which gourmets consider to be the best in France and which is recognised by its distinctive
yellow colour. This recipe comes from the Restaurant Auberge du Père Bise in Talloires.*

Serves 4

1 chicken, weighing 1.5 kg (3 lb)	**the chicken giblets**
salt and freshly ground black pepper	**4 tablespoons chicken stock**
1 bunch fresh tarragon	**4 tablespoons cream**
100 g (3½ oz) butter	

1. Season the inside of the chicken with salt and pepper and stuff it with the bunch of fresh tarragon.
2. Melt the butter in a heavy flameproof casserole dish, and gently cook the chicken until it is golden on all sides.
3. Add the giblets to the casserole dish.
4. Add the chicken stock, cover and cook very gently for about 40 minutes, or until the chicken is cooked through.
5. Remove the chicken from the casserole and keep warm.
6. Remove the bunch of tarragon from the chicken, return it to the casserole and continue cooking for a few minutes.
7. Add the cream, blend well and heat gently without allowing it to boil.
8. Strain the sauce through a fine sieve and correct the seasoning. It should be smooth, creamy and rather thin.
9. Cut the chicken into 4 serving pieces, coat each piece with the sauce and serve.

Terrine de Foie de Porc

Pork liver terrine

Serves 8

500 g (1 lb) pork liver	**salt and freshly ground black pepper**
250 g (8 oz) nut of veal	**2 tablespoons brandy**
250 g (8 oz) fresh lard	**3 eggs**
1 onion, chopped	**thin strips of lard to line the**
parsley	**terrine dish**
4¼ cups (8 oz) fresh breadcrumbs,	**sprig of thyme and bay leaf**
which have been soaked in cold	
milk, and squeezed in the hands	

1. Preheat the oven to 180°C (350°F).
2. Pound the pork liver, veal, lard, onion, parsley and breadcrumbs in a food processor, or food mill.
3. Season with salt and pepper.
4. Add the brandy and eggs, and mix together well.
5. Line a terrine dish with the thin strips of lard, and fill with the mixture.
6. Cover the top with the lard, and arrange the sprigs of thyme and the bay leaf decoratively on the top.
7. Cover the terrine, stand it in a dish of hot water, and place in the oven for 1¼ hours.
8. Remove from the oven and allow to cool for ½ hour.
9. Place a weight (about 1 kg) on top of the terrine, and leave it to set in the refrigerator overnight before serving.

Gratin de Queues d'Écrevisses

Crayfish tails in a cream sauce

Serves 4

1 kg (2 lb) live crayfish (green prawns
  may be substituted)
90 g (3 oz) butter
3 carrots, finely chopped
3 spring onions (scallions),
  finely chopped
½ cup (4 fl oz) brandy, warmed
½ cup (4 fl oz) dry white wine

1 tomato, peeled, seeded and chopped
1 sprig of thyme
½ bay leaf
salt and freshly ground black pepper
2 cups (16 fl oz) fresh cream
1 tablespoon soft butter
1 tablespoon flour

1. Wash the crayfish, or prawns and leave for a few minutes in very clean water. Gut them.
2. Heat the butter in a large saucepan, and add the carrots and spring onions.
3. Stew the vegetables gently, stirring, for 2 minutes.
4. Add the crayfish, cover the saucepan, and sauté for 5 minutes, shaking the pan.
5. Pour the warmed brandy into the pan and ignite.
6. Stir the brandy in well so that the crayfish thoroughly absorb the flavour.
7. Put out the flames by adding the wine.
8. Then add the chopped tomato and herbs.
9. Cover the saucepan again and simmer very gently for 5 minutes.
10. Remove the crayfish from the sauce, and detach the heads.
11. Crush the heads slightly and return them to the stock.
12. Cook the stock for a few more minutes to reduce it.
13. Add the cream and bring the sauce slowly back to the boil.
14. Strain the sauce through a very fine sieve into a small, heavy saucepan, pressing down hard to extract all the juices.
15. Heat the sauce.
16. Blend the tablespoon of butter with the tablespoon of flour to make a beurre manié.
17. Using a wire whisk, blend the beurre manié into the sauce, and keep whisking while it comes to the boil.
18. The sauce should be rich and smooth.
19. Correct the seasoning.
20. Shell the crayfish.
21. Spoon a layer of the hot sauce into the bottom of a cast-iron oven dish.
22. Arrange the crayfish on top and cover with the rest of the sauce.
23. Glaze under a very hot grill for about 2 minutes.
24. Serve immediately.

Gratin Dauphinois

Potatoes and cheese au gratin

Serves 4-6

1 clove garlic
1 kg (2 lb) potatoes, peeled and
  finely sliced
salt and freshly ground black pepper
250 g (8 oz) grated cheese

1 cup (8 fl oz) milk
1 egg
pinch of nutmeg
knob of butter

1. Preheat the oven to 180°C (350°F).
2. Rub a deep oven-proof dish with a clove of garlic.
3. Butter the dish well.
4. Line the bottom with a layer of potatoes.
5. Add some salt, pepper and a sprinkling of cheese.
6. Repeat the layers, potatoes, salt, pepper and cheese.
7. Pour in the milk, which has been beaten with the egg.
8. The potatoes should not be quite covered with milk.
9. Finish with grated nutmeg and cheese and dot with butter.
10. Bake for about 1 hour, or until the potatoes are cooked and the top is golden, and serve.

Râble de Lièvre à la Crème

Saddle of hare in cream sauce
This recipe comes from the Restaurant de Paris in Arbois.

Serves 4-6

100 g (3 oz) lard
2 saddles of hare
1 cup (8 fl oz) red wine
125 g (4 oz) butter
salt and freshly ground black pepper
¼ cup (2 fl oz) brandy
100 g (3 oz) spring onions (scallions),
  finely chopped

1 clove garlic, finely chopped
50 g (1½ oz) onions, finely chopped
50 g (1½ oz) carrots, finely chopped
1 bouquet garni
¼ cup (1 oz) flour
½ bottle red wine
½ cup (4 fl oz) cream

1. Lard the saddles of hare and marinate in the cup of red wine. (In cooler climates the hare would be marinated for up to 8 days; here a couple of days would be sufficient).
2. Remove the hare from the marinade and dry well.
3. Preheat the oven to 220°C (425°F).
4. Melt the butter in a heavy flameproof casserole, and brown the hare on all sides.
5. Season well with salt and freshly ground black pepper and cook in the oven for 6 minutes.
6. Remove the casserole from the oven, and flame the hare with the brandy, cooking until the flames have died away.
7. Remove the hare and keep it warm.
8. Add the chopped vegetables and bouquet garni to the casserole, and cook them until they are a golden colour.
9. Add the flour, and stir until a dark brown colour is obtained.
10. Moisten with the ½ bottle of red wine, stirring well to obtain a thick dark sauce.
11. Allow the sauce to cook and reduce for 10 minutes.
12. Add the cream.
13. Check the seasoning.
14. Strain the sauce.
15. Carve the hare into thin fillets.
16. Arrange on a serving dish, cover with the sauce and serve very hot. This dish may be served with mushrooms.

Tarte à l'Oignon

Onion tart

Serves 6-8

250 g (8 oz) short pastry (see p. 150)
60 g (2 oz) butter
250 g (8 oz) onions, chopped
3 eggs
2 egg yolks

pinch of grated nutmeg
salt and freshly ground black pepper
1 cup (8 fl oz) milk
1 cup (8 fl oz) cream

1. Preheat the oven to 200°C (400°F).
2. Prepare the short pastry.
3. Melt the butter in a heavy bottomed pan, and gently cook the onions until they are soft and golden. Cool.
4. In a mixing bowl, beat the eggs and egg yolks together with the nutmeg, salt and freshly ground pepper, milk and cream.
5. Add the drained onions and mix well.
6. Roll out the pastry to 5 mm (¼ in) thick and line a 20-25 cm (9-10 in) flan ring, standing on a baking sheet.
7. Pour the onion filling carefully into the flan case.
8. Bake in the preheated oven for about 40 minutes or until the filling is golden brown and set.
9. Serve either hot or cold.

Hotel Restaurant de Paris, Arbois.

If the smile of a chef is an indication of his greatness, André Jeunet is a giant. A friendly welcome awaits the guests at de Paris, where master chef Jeunet offers the finest dishes of the cuisine of the Franche-Comté. Not only a giant in the kitchen, M. Jeunet is enormous physically, yet with the help of his son, Jean-Paul, he prepares the most delicate Soufflé of Pike, Exquisite Canêton à l'Arboisienne and lush Gâteau au Chocolat. The Jeunet family keep one of the happiest and finest eating houses in France.

Above: *Saddle of Hare in Cream Sauce.*
Right: *Monsieur André Jeunet and his son Jean-Paul at their restaurant de Paris.*

Gâteau de Foies de Volailles à la Bressane

Chicken liver 'cake'

Serves 4-6

300 g (10 oz) chicken livers
75 g (2½ oz) flour
4 whole eggs
4 egg yolks
3 tablespoons cream
3 cups (24 fl oz) milk

salt and freshly ground black pepper
pinch of nutmeg
½ tablespoon parsley, very
**   finely chopped**
½ clove garlic, crushed

1. Preheat the oven to 160°C (325°F).
2. Press the chicken livers through a sieve into a bowl, or use a food processor to blend the livers.
3. Beat in the sieved flour with a whisk.
4. Add the whole eggs, one by one, working them in with a wooden spoon.
5. Add the egg yolks in a similar way.
6. Using the whisk, beat in the cream, then the milk, seasonings, parsley and garlic.
7. Work well until the mixture is nicely thickened and all the ingredients are blended. A food processor is ideal for this.
8. Pour the mixture into a round or rectangular terrine.
9. Place the terrine in a pan of water, letting the water come half way up the sides.
10. Bring to simmering point on top of the stove.
11. Transfer to the preheated oven.
12. Cook gently for 40-45 minutes.
13. Test by piercing with a needle. The juices should run clear, and the gâteau should start to come away from the sides of the mould.
14. Turn the gâteau out on to a warmed dish, and serve accompanied by a tomato sauce.

L'Omelette Savoyarde

Savoy omelette

Serves 4

4 canned artichoke hearts
125 g (4 oz) butter
4 medium sized potatoes, peeled
**   and diced**
4 leeks

8 eggs
salt and freshly ground black pepper
125 g (4 oz) Gruyère cheese, sliced
2 tablespoons parsley, finely chopped

1. Drain the artichoke hearts and dice.
2. Melt half the butter in a heavy saucepan.
3. Add the diced potatoes and artichoke hearts, cover and cook over a very low heat until they are tender.
4. Thoroughly wash the leeks and discard the green part.
5. Slice the white part into thin rounds and add to the potatoes and artichoke hearts when they are almost cooked.
6. Cook for a further 5 minutes until tender.
7. Season the eggs with salt and pepper and beat lightly.
8. Heat the remaining butter in a large omelette pan.
9. Add the Gruyère and parsley to the vegetables and mix.
10. Add the vegetable mixture to the eggs and pour into the omelette pan.
11. Cook until the eggs are lightly set and serve.

Fondue des Montagnes

Cheese Fondue
For this dish you will need a thick pan or a fondue dish to keep warm over a spirit lamp.

Serves 4-6

1 clove garlic
1 cup (8 fl oz) dry white wine
salt and white pepper

750 g (1½ lb) Gruyère cheese, sliced
1 tablespoon Kirsch
cubes of French bread, slightly stale

1. Rub a thick pan, or the fondue dish with the clove of garlic.
2. Pour the white wine into the pan with the salt and pepper.
3. Simmer the wine on the stove and add the cheese a little at a time, stirring constantly so that it gradually melts.
4. When all the cheese has melted, add the Kirsch. (If Kirsch is unavailable, brandy may be substituted.)
5. Transfer the pan to the spirit stove and place it in the middle of the table.
6. Each guest has a fondue fork and a pile of bread cubes, ready to dip into the gently bubbling cheese.

Mate Faims (Sucré)

Sweet Pancakes
The name of the dish is of Spanish origin, Mata-fame, which means it kills the hunger.

Serves 6

100 g (3½ oz) flour
50 g (1¾ oz) sugar
3 eggs
¾ cup (6 fl oz) milk

pinch salt
2 tablespoons oil
3 tablespoons Kirsch
50 g (1¾ oz) butter, melted

1. In a mixing bowl make a batter by combining the flour, sugar, eggs, milk, salt, oil, Kirsch and melted butter.
2. Let it rest for 1 hour in the refrigerator.
3. Brush a pancake pan with a little oil and add enough batter to make a fairly thick pancake.
4. Fry it on both sides.
5. Keep hot until all pancakes are cooked.
6. Serve them with gooseberry or strawberry jam.

Mousse aux Apricots

Apricot Mousse

Serves 6

375 g (12 oz) ripe apricots, peeled
  by plunging into boiling water,
  and stoned
6 tablespoons icing (confectioners)
  sugar

juice of half a lemon
30 g (1 oz) gelatine
1¼ cups (10 fl oz) cream, whipped

1. Purée the apricots in a blender or food processor.
2. Add the sugar and lemon juice.
3. Melt the gelatine in a little warm water and add it to the apricot mixture.
4. Thoroughly mix in the whipped cream.
5. Pour the mixture into individual dessert dishes, refrigerate and serve decorated with slices of apricot.

Provence, Côte d'Azur

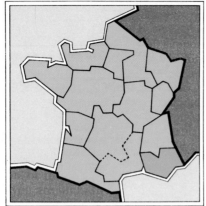

The list of dishes with the description 'à la Provençale' is indeed very long and varied. It denotes the use of tomato and garlic which, together with oil, form the main elements of the cuisine of Provence. Another ingredient or rather 'a handful of ingredients' are the herbes de Provence: rosemary, thyme, sage, bay leaves, parsley, oregano, fennel and many others. The combination of such basic ingredients gives the food of the Provence its characteristic fragrance.

People of the Provence eat well and hearty and they make the best of the intense flavours of the ingredients: the vegetables are renowned for their quality, the lamb is excellent (among the best-known dishes is Leg of Mutton Avignonnaise), while the most famous beef dish is the inimitable Daube de Boeuf à la Provençal. Local fruit such as figs or watermelon are the usual and most perfect way of ending a Provençal meal.

The French Riviera is part of Provence but geographically cut off from the rest. It has developed its own style of cooking. Even today there seems to be reluctance in the interior of the Provence to eat seafish except in its traditional dried form, while along the coast from Marseilles to Menton on the Italian border, fish and seafood are the glory of the cooking of the Côte d'Azur, and the Bouillabaisse its apotheosis. There seems to be no general agreement on the ingredients and there are as many versions as there are cooks along the rocky winding coast. Ancient Greek literature speaks of a Bouillabaisse-type dish and today many parts of France have their own variations: in Brittany you will encounter the Cotriade, in Poitou they serve Chaudrée and in Burgundy the Pauchouse.

One thing is certain, it's the day's catch which determines what goes into the Bouillabaisse, so in some places you will find Bouillabaisse de Sardines or de Morue (with salt cod) and even a dish locally called Bouillabaisse d'Epinard, a type of spinach-potato-egg bubble and squeak.

The further east one goes along the coast the more the Italian influence can be felt. So that in Nice, one finds that dishes such as Gnocchis à la Nicoise and Ravioli are considered a local speciality.

Bay near St. Tropez.

Soupe au Pistou

A very popular soup, lightly flavoured with sweet basil

Serves 6-8

125 g (4 oz) dried haricot beans
125 g (4 oz) dried kidney beans
250 g (8 oz) green beans, chopped
  in half
1 large onion, chopped
250 g (8 oz) carrots, chopped
250 g (8 oz) zucchinis (courgettes),
  chopped

250 g (8 oz) tomatoes, peeled
  and chopped
250 g (8 oz) small noodles
2 cloves garlic
1½ tablespoons fresh basil
2 tablespoons olive oil
salt

1. Soak the white haricot beans and red kidney beans in water for 2 to 3 hours. Drain.
2. Place the chopped beans, onion, carrots, zucchinis and tomatoes in a large saucepan.
3. Add the dried beans and cover with plenty of salted water.
4. Bring to the boil, and simmer for 1½ hours.
5. Add the noodles to the simmering stock and continue cooking for a further 5 to 10 minutes.
6. While the soup is cooking, crush the garlic in a mortar with plenty of green basil leaves.
7. Add the olive oil to the mortar and mix to a paste.
8. When the vegetables are cooked, add a scoop of the hot soup to the garlic, basil and oil paste. Mix well, and return to the soup.
9. Bring to the boil, and serve, accompanied by rounds of French bread, olive oil and some grated cheese.

Aioli Garni

This dish, very popular in Provence, is composed of vegetables, eggs, and fish, decoratively arranged and served with aioli sauce.

Serves 6

500 g (1 lb) salt codfish
12 small new potatoes in their jackets
6 small sweet potatoes in their jackets
6 zucchinis (courgettes)
500 g (1 lb) small carrots
500 g (1 lb) French beans
6 eggs
6 ripe tomatoes, peeled and cut
  into wedges

lettuce
fresh herbs such as parsley, basil
  to garnish

Aioli sauce:
4 cloves garlic per person
1 egg yolk per two persons
olive oil
salt and freshly ground black pepper
lemon juice

1. Soak the codfish overnight in cold water.
2. Simmer the fish in fresh water for about 10 minutes until cooked. Drain well.
3. Steam all the vegetables separately until they are cooked, but still quite firm; on no account should they be overcooked.
4. Hard-boil the eggs and cut in half.
5. Take a large round serving dish and place the fish in the centre, surrounded by the hot vegetables, hard-boiled eggs and raw tomatoes, decorated with lettuce and sprigs of fresh herbs. Serve with aioli sauce, from which this famous dish gets its name.

Aioli Sauce:
1. Take 4 cloves of garlic per person and 1 egg yolk for each two persons.
2. Crush the garlic to a smooth paste in a mortar with a little salt, or use a food processor.
3. Blend in the egg yolks until the mixture is a smooth homogeneous mass.
4. Whisk the olive oil into the egg mixture, at first drop by drop, then in a thin trickle, as you would for a mayonnaise.
5. The aioli will thicken gradually until it reaches the proper stiff, firm consistency. (The exact quantity of oil is determined by the number of egg yolks used, but the sauce should resemble a firm mayonnaise.)
6. Season to taste with salt, freshly ground black pepper and lemon juice. The sauce is served chilled.

Soupe de Poisson au Vermicelle à la Marseillaise

Fish soup with vermicelli à la Marseillaise

Serves 6-8

Soup:
6 tablespoons olive oil
2 onions, finely chopped
4-5 cloves garlic, crushed
1 kg (2 lb) small rockfish, cleaned,
   or selection of fish heads
   and trimmings
2 tablespoons tomato paste
10 cups (2.5 litres) water
bouquet garni
salt and freshly ground black pepper
2 potatoes, peeled and chopped
pinch of powdered saffron
60 g (2 oz) broken spaghetti,
   or vermicelli

Rouille:
2 cloves garlic
2 egg yolks
6 tablespoons olive oil
½ teaspoon powdered saffron
salt and freshly ground black pepper

To serve:
French bread, sliced in rounds and
   lighly toasted
grated Gruyère or Cheddar

Soup:
1. Heat the oil in a large saucepan, and sauté the onions and garlic until soft and transparent.
2. Add the fish and the tomato paste, and cook, stirring, for 2 minutes.
3. Pour in the water and bring to the boil. Add the bouquet garni, salt, freshly ground black pepper and potatoes. Simmer for 30 minutes.
4. Strain the soup into another pan, pressing as much fish as possible through the sieve.
5. Add the saffron and check the seasoning, adding more salt if necessary.
6. Bring to the boil, stir in the spaghetti and simmer for 10 minutes.
7. While the soup is simmering, make the rouille.

Rouille:
1. Beat together the garlic and the egg yolks.
2. Whisk in the oil, drop by drop as for a mayonnaise.
3. Add the saffron, and season with salt and pepper.

To Serve:
1. Spread the toast generously with the rouille, and sprinkle some grated cheese on top.
2. Ladle the soup into dishes and garnish with the toast.

Soupe de Campagne

Country Soup

Serves 6-8

3 tablespoons olive oil
3 onions, finely chopped
2 leeks, finely chopped
6 tomatoes, peeled, seeded
   and chopped

6 cups (1.5 litres) beef stock
salt and freshly ground black pepper
1½ cups (6 oz) grated cheese
fresh black bread to serve

1. Heat the olive oil in a large heavy saucepan and gently cook the onions and leeks until they are soft but not coloured.
2. Add the tomatoes and continue cooking until the mixture is like a thick sauce.
3. Add the stock and season well.
4. Bring to the boil and add the grated cheese
5. Simmer gently for about 30 minutes.
6. Serve accompanied by fresh black bread.

La Bouillabaisse

Bouillabaisse, or fish chowder
There is no general agreement on the ingredients for this dish, each locality varies and the final choice depends upon the catch of the day.

Serves 6-8

Soup:
6 tablespoons olive oil
2 medium onions, finely chopped
1 leek, chopped
½ stalk fennel, chopped
2 medium tomatoes, peeled, seeded
  and chopped
3 cloves garlic, crushed
generous sprig of thyme
1 bay leaf
1 celery stalk, chopped
1.75 kg (3½ lb) coarse-fleshed fish,
  such as cod, mullet, mackerel etc.

12 cups (3 litres) white wine fish fumet
  (see p. 149)
salt and freshly ground black pepper
1 teaspoon powdered saffron
1.75 kg (3½ lb) fine-fleshed fish,
  such as snapper, whiting, sole,
  John Dory etc.
garlic flavoured croûtons

Rouille:
2 cloves garlic, crushed
2 small green peppers
2 egg yolks
6 tablespoons olive oil

Soup:
1. Heat 4 tablespoons of the olive oil in a large fireproof casserole dish or fish kettle.
2. Add the onions, leek and fennel and cook them gently over a very low heat until the onion is tender, but not browned.
3. Add the tomatoes, garlic, thyme, bay leaf and celery, and cook for a few minutes longer.
4. Remove the heads from the fish, clean and trim them.
5. Add the coarse-fleshed fish and the fish stock to the vegetables.
6. Season with salt and freshly ground black pepper and the saffron.
7. Bring to the boil and cook over a brisk heat for 6 minutes.
8. Add the rest of the fish and continue cooking over a brisk heat for another 6 minutes, or until all the fish are cooked. Take great care not to overcook the fish.
9. Lift out the fish with a slotted spoon and put into a large warmed serving bowl. Sprinkle with the remaining 2 tablespoons of oil.
10. Pour the stock into a soup tureen, and put the garlic croûtons in a separate bowl.

Rouille:
1. Crush the garlic with the green peppers in a mortar, or food processor.
2. Add the egg yolks, and beat in the oil as for a mayonnaise.
3. Season to taste with salt and freshly ground black pepper.
4. Finish with a tablespoon of the hot fish broth, beaten in with a wire whisk.
5. Serve in a sauceboat with the rest of the bouillabaisse. Serve the fish separately.

Pistou

Basil, garlic and Parmesan sauce
This sauce is related to the Italian pesto and with minor variations is prepared right along the Provençal coast. It is stirred into soups, pasta or bouillabaisse.

4 cloves garlic (use less if preferred)
4 tablespoons tomato paste
6 tablespoons chopped fresh basil

½ cup (2 oz) grated Parmesan
⅔ cup (5 fl oz) olive oil

1. Place the garlic, tomato paste, basil and cheese in a large mortar and crush with a pestle until you have a fine paste.
2. Add the oil, drop by drop, as you would for mayonnaise.
3. If you have a food processor, place all the ingredients except the oil into the work bowl and process until it is smooth. Gradually add the oil while continuing to process.

Chez Fonfon, Marseilles.

Unless one knows where to look while driving along the Corniche President J. F. Kennedy, it is easy to miss Vallon des Auffes, and that would be a pity, for it is one of the few remaining fishing ports in Marseilles. You can still see the fishermen tying up their boats and tending their nets as they have done for centuries. Around the water, their houses hug closely together. Chez Fonfon is one of these houses, overlooking the tiny bay. Here the patron Alphonse Mouiner delights his guests with the freshest seafood in Marseilles, and he has the reputation of preparing one of the best bouillabaisse — not an easy task in a town where that dish is king.

Above: *Ingredients of Bouillabaisse as prepared at Chez Fonfon.*

Estouffade de Boeuf de Carmargue

Beef casserole

Serves 6-8

375 g (12 oz) lean bacon, diced
30 g (1 oz) + 1 tablespoon butter
3 tablespoons olive oil
2 kg (4 lb) lean beef
3 tablespoons flour
8 medium-sized onions, quartered
500 g (1 lb) tomatoes, peeled, seeded
   and chopped

salt and freshly ground black pepper
3½ cups (1 bottle) red wine
well flavoured beef stock, to cover
2 cloves garlic, crushed
30 black olives
bouquet garni
375 g (12 oz) mushrooms, sliced

1. Preheat the oven to 120°C (250°F).
2. Blanch the diced bacon in boiling water for 2 minutes.
3. Melt 30 g of the butter and the oil in a large heavy pan, and fry the drained bacon until golden.
4. Remove the bacon from the pan.
5. Cut the beef into good sized chunks.
6. Sprinkle the meat with flour and brown in the butter, oil and bacon fat.
7. Add the onions to the meat chunks and cook, stirring constantly, until they are well browned. Add the tomatoes and continue cooking.
8. Season with salt and pepper.
9. Add the wine and stock to cover.
10. Add the garlic, olives and bouquet garni.
11. Cook, covered, in the oven, for about 2½ to 3 hours.
12. Drain the meat into a tin sieve placed over a clean saucepan.
13. Place the beef chunks and bacon cubes in a clean casserole.
14. Melt the remaining butter in a clean frying pan and sauté the mushrooms for 2 minutes.
15. Add the mushrooms to the meat.
16. Skim the fat from the sauce.
17. Reduce the sauce over a high flame until it is the desired consistency, and strain it over the meat.
18. Simmer gently, covered for a further 30 minutes, or until tender.
19. Serve from the casserole.

Les Écrevisses Flambées aux Herbes de Provence

Crayfish flambé with herbs.
King prawns may be substituted for crayfish.

Serves 6

30 raw crayfish, or king prawns
4 tablespoons olive oil
salt and freshly ground black pepper
1 tablespoon finely chopped fennel
1 tablespoon finely chopped rosemary
   and thyme

2 cloves garlic, crushed
2 tablespoons parsley, finely chopped
5 juniper berries, crushed
3 tablespoons brandy, warmed
1¼ cups (10 fl oz) dry white wine

1. Peel and gut the crayfish, or king prawns.
2. Heat the oil in a large heavy frying pan and sauté the crayfish or prawns over a brisk heat until they are done (about 7-10 minutes, depending on the size).
3. Season them with salt and pepper while they are cooking.
4. Add the herbs, garlic and juniper berries, stirring well.
5. Pour over the warmed brandy and ignite.
6. When the flames have died down, add the wine.
7. Cook over a brisk heat for one or two minutes.
8. Stir and serve immediately.

Brochettes de Moules, Sauce Provençale

Mussels and bacon on a skewer, with sauce Provençale

Serves 4

1 kg (2 lb) mussels
4 slices bacon, cut into 4 squares
1 egg yolk, beaten with
  1 tablespoon milk
fresh breadcrumbs
sprig of fresh thyme
olive oil
salt and freshly ground black pepper
1 lemon, cut into quarters

Provençale Sauce:
1 kg (2 lb) tomatoes, peeled, seeded
  and chopped
3 tablespoons olive oil
bouquet garni
1 clove garlic, crushed
salt and freshly ground black pepper

1. Scrub the mussels, and put them in a deep cast-iron saucepan over a high heat without adding any liquid.
2. Cover the pan.
3. As soon as the shells open, remove them from the shell.
4. Thread them on a skewer, two at a time, inserting a piece of bacon between each pair.
5. Each skewer should consist of 4 pieces of bacon and 10 mussels.
6. Dip the skewers in the diluted egg yolks.
7. Roll the skewers in the breadcrumbs, and set aside.
8. To make the sauce, cook the tomatoes in the olive oil with the bouquet garni for 35 to 40 minutes.
9. When cooked, add the garlic, and season with salt and pepper.
10. To cook the mussels, brush the skewers with a sprig of thyme, dipped in olive oil.
11. Place under a very hot grill, turning to cook evenly.
12. Do not let the mussels blacken. They should be dry and well browned.
13. Transfer the skewers to a heated dish, and garnish with lemon quarters. Serve the sauce separately.

Oeufs Tapenade

Hard-boiled eggs stuffed with anchovies, olives and capers
The name for this simple yet tasty dish is taken from 'Tapèno', the Provençal dialect for capers.

Serves 6

6 hard-boiled eggs
30 g (1 oz) black olives, stoned
8 anchovy fillets
30 g (1 oz) tinned tuna fish
3 tablespoons capers

6 tablespoons olive oil
lemon juice
2 teaspoons brandy
freshly ground black pepper
a few sprigs of parsley to garnish

1. Halve the hard-boiled eggs lengthwise and carefully scoop out the yolks. Reserve.
2. Using a pestle and mortar, or a food processor, pound the olives, anchovies, tuna and capers to a smooth paste.
3. Beat in the oil, a little at a time, until the mixture is a creamy, thick consistency.
4. Mash the egg yolks and blend into the mixture.
5. Add a little lemon juice, the brandy and black pepper to taste.
6. Place in a piping bag, and pipe the stuffing into the hollow egg whites.
7. Garnish with sprigs of parsley, and serve on a bed of lettuce leaves, as a first course or part of an hors d'oeuvre.

Des Culs d'Artichauts Violets, Ris de Veau et Foie d'Oie

Artichoke bottoms, sweetbreads and goose livers
This recipe comes from Le Petit Nice in Marseilles.

Serves 4

4-8 artichokes, depending on size
½ teaspoon salt
water sufficient to cover artichokes
1 lemon
2 sweetbreads
1 cup (8 fl oz) dry white wine

2 tablespoons fresh cream
2-3 goose livers, depending on size
  (or 350 g (11 oz) chicken livers)
2 tablespoons butter
salt
freshly ground pepper

1. Trim the artichokes and remove the tough external leaves, cut the top of the leaves flat and remove the stalk.
2. Boil the artichoke hearts in salted water to which the juice of the lemon has been added. Cook for 10 minutes.
3. In another pan of water blanch the sweetbreads for 5-8 minutes. Remove and save the water.
4. Rinse the sweetbreads under cold running water and remove the external skin.
5. Chop the sweetbreads finely.
6. To the water in which the sweetbreads were cooked add the white wine and cook until it has been reduced to about one quarter of its volume, enough sauce for four people. Add the cream.
7. Clean the goose livers, cut them into thin slices and trim them into pieces approximately 4 cm x 4 cm (1½ in x 1½ in).
8. In a frying pan, melt the butter and very briefly sauté the goose livers in it. Season with pepper and salt.
9. To assemble, spread the leaves of the artichoke, if necessary remove the choke, and in between the leaves place the chopped sweetbreads.
10. To serve, arrange the goose liver squares on a plate, place the artichokes on top of the livers and mask the artichokes with the sauce. Serve immediately.

Note: If fresh artichokes are not available, use canned artichoke hearts. In this case, blanch the sweetbreads in the water from the can.

Pissaladière

Savoury tart with onions, olives, grated cheese and anchovy fillets

Serves 6-8

250 g (8 oz) shortcrust pastry (see p. 150)
2 tablespoons olive oil
3 large onions, finely sliced
12 black olives

60 g (2 oz) achovy fillets
125 g (4 oz) grated cheese
  (Gruyère or Cheddar)

1. Preheat the oven to 210°C (420°F).
2. Prepare the shortcrust pastry.
3. Heat the oil in a heavy bottomed frying pan, and cook the finely sliced onions gently until they are soft but still transparent.
4. Roll out the pastry and line a 30 cm (12 in) shallow pie tin.
5. Top the pastry with the cooked onions.
6. Decorate with anchovies and olives.
7. Sprinkle the cheese over the whole tart.
8. Bake until the pastry is cooked and the tart is golden on top (approximately 20 minutes).
9. Serve hot.

Le Petit Nice, Marseilles.
Overlooking the Bay of Marseilles and Château d'If, the fortress prison made famous by Dumas in his story of the Count of Monte Cristo, Le Petit Nice is a place of comfort, refinement and good food. As you would expect in Marseilles, the best dishes on the menu are seafood. Chef Jean Paul Passedat has an orginal touch, and while he uses purely local ingredients, he comes up with some very unusual combinations.

Above: *Artichoke hearts, sweetbreads and goose liver as prepared at Le Petit Nice in Marseilles.*

Lapin à la Niçoise

Rabbit with tomatoes and peppers

Serves 4-6

1 rabbit, weighing 1.5-2 kg (3-4 lb)
  jointed
3 tablespoons olive oil
185 g (6 oz) salted pork belly, diced
3 medium onions, sliced
1 red pepper, cored, seeded and sliced
1 green pepper, cored, seeded
  and sliced

500 g (1 lb) tomatoes, peeled, seeded
  and chopped
2 tablespoons chopped mixed herbs
  (thyme, basil, parsley)
2 teaspoons French mustard
salt and freshly ground black pepper

1. Preheat the oven to 160°C (325°F).
2. Wash and dry the rabbit pieces thoroughly.
3. Heat the oil in a heavy bottomed pan, and fry the diced pork belly briskly, until evenly browned.
4. Transfer the pork to a large casserole.
5. Add the rabbit to the frying pan, and brown on all sides in the hot oil.
6. Transfer the rabbit pieces to the casserole.
7. Fry the onions and peppers in the oil remaining in the pan until soft but not browned.
8. Add the tomatoes, herbs and mustard, bring to the boil and pour over the meats.
9. Season to taste with salt and freshly ground black pepper.
10. Cover and cook in the oven, for about 1¼ hours, or until the rabbit is tender.

Fricassée Provençale

A typically Provençale chicken fricassée
The chicken is combined with a mixture of garlic, almonds and bread soaked in vinegar and the sauce is thickened with a strongly lemon flavoured mayonnaise.

Serves 4

Provençale base:
4 tablespoons olive oil
1 head garlic, each clove peeled
60 g (2 oz) almonds, blanched
75 g (2½ oz) white bread, in one piece,
  soaked in while wine vinegar and
  squeezed dry
salt and freshly ground black pepper

½ bay leaf
1 chicken, about 1.5 to 2 kg (3-4 lb)
  jointed
1 cup (8 fl oz) chicken stock
¾ cup (6 fl oz) mayonnaise, well
  flavoured with lemon
finely chopped parsley

1. Heat the olive oil in a heavy bottomed pan, and gently cook the garlic cloves, almonds, bread and bay leaf for 2 to 3 minutes, until they start to take on a little colour.
2. Remove all these ingredients from the oil, draining them to leave as much oil in the pan as possible.
3. Dry the chicken pieces, put them in the oil and cook them for about 15 minutes, turning them from time to time so that they become an even colour.
4. Using a mortar, or a food processor, reduce the base to a paste.
5. In a small saucepan, reduce the chicken stock over a brisk heat until ½ cup remains.
6. Thin the provençal paste with the concentrated chicken stock, and add this sauce to the chicken pieces in the frying pan.
7. Cover the pan and finish cooking over a moderate heat for 20 to 25 minutes.
8. Remove the chicken pieces from the pan and keep warm.
9. Remove the pan from the fire and thicken the sauce by beating in the mayonnaise with a wire whisk, a little at a time.
10. Return the chicken pieces to the sauce, and keep warm by standing the pan in a dish of boiling water.
11. The sauce must not boil, or it will curdle.
12. Transfer the chicken and the sauce to a deep serving dish, and serve sprinkled with freshly chopped parsley.

Thon à la Provençale

Tuna fish à la Provençal

Serves 6

Marinade:
3 tablespoons olive oil
1 tablespoon lemon juice
salt and freshly ground black pepper
6 tuna steaks
3 anchovy fillets
3 tablespoons olive oil
1 onion, finely chopped

3 large tomatoes, peeled, seeded
  and chopped
1 clove garlic, crushed
bouquet garni
¾ cup (6 fl oz) dry white wine
30 g (1 oz) butter, soft
1 tablespoon flour
1 teaspoon capers

1. Mix the oil, lemon juice, salt and freshly ground black pepper together to make a marinade.
2. Stud each tuna steak with half an anchovy fillet, cut in small pieces.
3. Place the tuna steaks in the marinade for at least an hour.
4. Preheat the oven to 150°C (300°F).
5. Heat the rest of the oil in a large ovenproof dish.
6. Soften the chopped onion in the oil.
7. Add the drained fish and cook it for a couple of minutes, allowing it to colour a little on both sides.
8. Add the tomatoes, garlic and bouquet garni.
9. Season with salt and feshly ground black pepper.
10. Pour the wine over the fish.
11. Transfer the pan to the oven, cover it and cook for about 15-20 minutes, or until the tuna is cooked.
12. Remove the fish from the pan, drain, and set on a warmed serving dish. Keep warm.
13. Blend the butter and flour together to make a beurre manié.
14. Whisk this into the sauce to thicken it.
15. Add the capers and simmer the sauce gently for a couple of minutes.
16. Pour the sauce carefully over the tuna steaks, and serve immediately.

Aubergines et Tomates au Gratin

Eggplant and tomato casserole

Serves 6-8

6 medium eggplants
salt and freshly ground black pepper
2 tablespoons olive oil
8 tablespoons grated Parmesan

¾ cup (6 fl oz) cream
6 large tomatoes, peeled and sliced
6 tablespoons dry breadcrumbs
30 g (1 oz) butter

1. Peel the eggplants, cut in thin slices and sprinkle with salt.
2. Let them 'sweat' in a dish for 2 hours, then drain.
3. Preheat the oven to 180°C (350°F).
4. Wipe the eggplant slices dry.
5. Heat the olive oil in a heavy pan, and fry the eggplant slices until they are soft and golden. Drain.
6. Butter a deep ovenproof casserole dish.
7. Place a layer of eggplant slices in the bottom and season with salt and freshly ground black pepper.
8. Sprinkle generously with Parmesan cheese and fresh cream.
9. Add a layer of sliced raw tomatoes, then add pepper, a little more cream and cheese.
10. Put another layer of eggplant slices on top and continue in this way until the dish is full.
11. Pour the remaining cream on top.
12. Cover the cream with breadcrumbs and grated Parmesan. Dot with butter.
13. Bake for about 45 minutes and serve from the casserole dish.

Daube Niçoise

Braised Steak Niçoise
This recipe comes from Restaurant L'Académia in Nice.

Serves 8

2 kg (4 lb) shin of beef
salt and freshly ground black pepper
olive oil
300 g (10 oz) onions, sliced
3 pieces garlic, crushed

4 cups (1 litre) red wine
500 g (1 lb) tomatoes, peeled
4 cups (1 litre) beef stock
500 g (1 lb) carrots, cut lengthwise
200 g (6 oz) mushrooms

1. Preheat the oven to 150°C (300°F).
2. Cut the beef into cubes of about 3 cm (1¼ in) and season with salt and pepper.
3. Heat the olive oil in a heavy pan and cook the beef, shaking the pan regularly, until the meat has taken on a golden colour.
4. Add the chopped onions and allow to brown with the meat.
5. Add the garlic, wine and peeled tomatoes, mix well.
6. Add 1 litre of beef stock, or water and check seasoning.
7. Cover, and cook in a slow oven for 3 hours.
8. Add the carrots and mushrooms to the beef and cook for a further 20 minutes.
9. Recheck the seasoning and serve.

Artichauts à la Barigoule

Artichokes stuffed with mushrooms, anchovies and ham, and cooked with olive oil, dry white wine, garlic and thyme

Serves 6

6 medium sized artichokes
½ cup (4 fl oz) olive oil
1 large onion, finely chopped
1 large carrot, finely sliced
a generous sprig of thyme
1 bay leaf
4 cloves garlic, crushed
salt and freshly ground black pepper
2 cups (16 fl oz) white wine
1 lemon

Stuffing:
30 g (1 oz) butter
250 g (8 oz) mushrooms, chopped
6 anchovy fillets, finely chopped
250 g (8 oz) sliced ham, very
**   finely chopped**
125 g (4 oz) lean bacon slices, cut in
**   3 cm (1¼ in) strips**

1. Cut the stalks off the artichokes and pull out the lower leaves.
2. Cut off the tops of the leaves with scissors.
3. Cut out the chokes.
4. Wash the artichokes in plenty of water with a few drops of lemon juice in it. Turn them upside down and drain.
5. To make the stuffing, melt the butter and gently cook the chopped mushrooms for a few minutes until they are soft.
6. Combine the mushrooms, anchovy fillets, ham and bacon in a bowl and mix thoroughly.
7. Stuff the artichokes with this mixture.
8. In a large casserole dish, heat the oil and gently cook the onion and carrot until they start to take on some colour.
9. Add the thyme, bay leaf and garlic.
10. Place the stuffed artichokes upright on top of the vegetables.
11. Season lightly.
12. Pour over the white wine and enough water to come up to the top of the artichokes.
13. Bring it to the boil, cover, and continue to simmer gently for about 40 minutes, or until the artichokes are tender and the cooking liquid is thick and smooth.
14. If the liquid seems a little thin, remove the artichokes to a warmed, deep serving dish.
15. Cook the sauce over a brisk heat until it is reduced to the desired consistency. Add a squeeze of lemon, pour the sauce around the artichokes and serve.

Restaurant L'Académia, Nice.
L'Académia is the seat of Culinary Academy of Nice. It has been established for many years and, according to a plaque on the building, Napoleon stayed there. The menu is typical of so many restaurants on the Côte d'Azure in that it is part Provençal, part Italian. You will find Caillette Provençale and Champignons à la Provençale right next to Ravioli à la Niçoise and Pissaladière, a close relation to the Italian pizza.

Above: *Braised Steak Niçoise (opposite page) as prepared at L'Académia in Nice.*

Gigot d'Agneau en Croûte

Stuffed leg of lamb in pastry
This exquisite dish is from the famous Baumanière Restaurant at les Beaux-en-Provence near Arles.

Serves 6

1.5 kg (3 lb) boned leg of lamb
2 lamb kidneys, cubed
¼ cup chopped mushrooms
60 g (2 oz) pâté de fois gras, mashed
1 tablespoon chopped truffles
  (optional)

2 tablespoons Armagnac or brandy
salt
freshly ground pepper
puff pastry (p. 150)
egg wash made from 1 egg and
  1 tablespoon of water

1. Preheat the oven to 165°C (325°F).
2. In a bowl combine the kidneys, mushrooms, pâté, truffles, Armagnac or brandy, salt and pepper.
3. Fill the cavity in the leg of lamb with the stuffing and either using skewers or string, close the opening.
4. Roast the leg for 45 minutes.
5. Remove it from the oven and allow it to cool slightly.
6. Increase the oven temperature to 220°C (425°F).
7. Roll out the dough to 6 mm (¼ in) thick.
8. Wrap the leg in the dough. Use left over dough to decorate the top with pastry leaves.
9. Brush the dough with egg wash and bake in the hot oven for 15-20 minutes or until the pastry is golden brown.
10. Remove it from oven and let it stand for 5 minutes.
11. To serve, carefully carve into slices making sure that each slice has a pastry crust.
12. Traditionally the dish is served with gratin dauphinois (scalloped potatoes).

Ratatouille Provençale

A delicious ragoût of summer vegetables, flavoured with herbs and garlic, which may be served either hot or cold
It will go equally well with a roast or casserole dish, or served with poached eggs on top. Left-over ratatouille makes a good filling for an omelette.

Serves 8-10

olive oil
1 kg (2 lb) eggplant (aubergine) peeled,
  seeded and chopped
500 g (1 lb) zucchinis, (courgettes)
  chopped
500 g (1 lb) green peppers, diced
3 onions, thinly sliced
750 g (1½ lb) tomatoes, peeled, seeded
  and crushed

bouquet garni
large sprig of thyme
1 whole head of garlic, with the cloves
  skinned and crushed.
salt and freshly ground black pepper
3 tablespoons fresh tarragon,
  finely chopped

1. Pour a thin layer of oil into a heavy frying pan.
2. Lightly fry the eggplant, zucchinis and green peppers, one after the other, transferring them to a dish as they are done.
3. Pour off the cooking oil and wipe the pan.
4. Pour in a thin layer of fresh olive oil.
5. Return the vegetables to the pan, adding the onions, tomatoes, bouquet garni, thyme and crushed garlic.
6. Season with salt and freshly ground black pepper.
7. Cover the pan and cook over a low heat for 1 hour, stirring from time to time.
8. Add another 1 or 2 tablespoons of oil if necessary, and 2 or 3 tablespoons of boiling water, but take care not to make the mixture too watery.
9. Half way through the cooking, stir in the chopped tarragon.
10. Serve hot or cold in a deep dish.

Soufflé aux Fruits Frais de Provence

Strawberry and Peach Soufflé

Serves 4

2 large ripe peaches
400 g (13 oz) small strawberries
½ cup (4 fl oz) Grand Marnier
4 egg yolks

100 g (3⅓ oz) caster (powdered) sugar
4 egg whites
pinch of salt
icing (confectioners) sugar

1. Preheat oven to 200°C (400°F).
2. Pour boiling water over the peaches then peel them. Cut them in halves, remove the stones and chop the flesh into small dice.
3. In a bowl, combine the diced peaches, the strawberries and the Grand Marnier and marinate for 2-3 hours. (If small strawberries are not available, cut large ones in halves or quarters).
4. In a mixing bowl, cream the egg yolks and the sugar until they are pale and creamy.
5. Mix the fruit and liquid into the yolk mixture.
6. Beat the egg whites with a pinch of salt until they are stiff.
7. Gently fold the egg whites into the yolk-fruit mixture.
8. Butter four small soufflé dishes and sprinkle the inside with sugar.
9. Fill the dishes and bake for approximately 15 minutes or until they have risen and are golden brown on top.
10. Serve immediately sprinkled with icing sugar.

Tourte à la Frangipane

Almond tart
A traditional Christmas sweet from Provence.

1 — 20 cm (8 in) tart

250 g (8 oz) puff pastry (see p. 150)
1⅔ cups (6 oz) ground almonds
¾ cup (6 oz) caster (powdered) sugar
1 egg

finely grated orange rind
3 tablespoons milk
1 egg, beaten with a little milk

1. Preheat the oven to 200°C (400°F).
2. Prepare the puff pastry.
3. In a saucepan, mix the ground almonds, sugar, egg and grated orange rind.
4. Add the milk so that you have a thick creamy consistency.
5. Cook gently, stirring, until the first bubbles rise.
6. Line a tart tin with half the pastry.
7. Cover with the almond paste.
8. Roll out the remaining pastry and cover the tin, crimping the edges.
9. Coat the top of the tart with the beaten egg and milk.
10. Bake for about 25 minutes or until the pastry is cooked.

Figues de Marseilles au Miel

Green figs in wine and honey

Serves 6-8

1 kg (2 lb) fresh green figs
white wine to cover

1 cup (12 oz) honey
fresh cream, whipped

1. Wash the figs, and place them in a saucepan with enough white wine to just cover them.
2. Bring the pan gently to the boil.
3. Add the honey.
4. Simmer for about 15 minutes, or until the figs are tender but still firm.
5. Chill the figs well in the liquid.
6. Serve very cold with whipped cream.

The Central Plateau and Languedoc

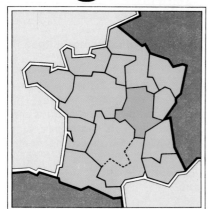

The climate of the Central Plateau has played an important part in shaping not only the landscape and its people but also the type of food eaten in the region.

This mountainous area, rugged in character, with hot summers and cold winters has produced a tough and hardy race used to the simple but good things in life. The country grows basic products of high quality and the food of the region is plain and hearty, and as in most areas where the people work hard and the winters are severe, it is fairly fatty.

The lamb is exceptionally tasty and has the flavour of the herbs on which the sheep feed. Pork is plentiful and lard is the chief cooking fat.

Many of the most characteristic dishes are made with either cabbage or potatoes or sometimes both. The region is also well known for its terrines, sausages and pâtés.

Geographically, the Perigord is part of the Central Plateau and while its cuisine is still basically of peasant origin, it has acquired some refinements from the Bordeaux region, its neighbour to the west. The most famous products of the Perigord are undoubtedly goose foie gras and truffles. The cooking of dishes 'à la Perigourdine' implies the use of either or both of these great ingredients. There are many Perigourdine recipes for cooking geese, but probably the best known is confit of goose where the goose meat, which is locally available in great quantities, is cooked and preserved under a seal of its own fat.

One of the most interesting regions from the gastronomic point of view is Languedoc, a large area to the south of the Central Plateau. Its food has been influenced by ancient Greek and Roman cooking as well as Arabic. The Couscous of North Africa is a relation of the Cassoulet of the Languedoc. Having direct access to the Mediterranean, the Languedoc cuisine includes a large number of seafood dishes. Many of them are similar to those of Provence, its neighbour along the coast. It even has two types of Bouillabaisse, one made with cod and the other with sardines. Mussels, anchovies and tuna are prepared in the manner of the dishes of Provence.

Château de Mercues, near Cahors

Bréjauda

Cabbage soup with bacon

Serves 8

500 g (1 lb) stewing lamb, diced
125 g (4 oz) lean bacon, diced
10 cups (2.5 litres) water
125 g (4 oz) carrots, finely sliced
4 medium onions, sliced

1 parsnip, sliced
1 leek, washed and sliced
500 g firm cabbage, cut into 8 pieces
4 medium potatoes, quartered
salt and freshly ground black pepper

1. Bring the diced meat and bacon to the boil in the water in a large pot.
2. Skim the pot well.
3. Add the vegetables, except for the cabbage and the potatoes. Season well with salt and pepper.
4. Simmer for 1 hour, or until the meat is cooked.
5. Add the potatoes and cabbage to the pot and simmer for a further 20 minutes, or until the potatoes and cabbage are cooked.
6. Serve in deep soup bowls.

Sardine Bouillabaisse

A rich bouillabaisse made only with sardines

Serves 6-8

1.5-2 kg (3-4 lb) fresh sardines
4 medium onions, finely chopped
500 g (1 lb) tomatoes, peeled
  and chopped
2 cloves garlic, finely chopped
sliver of orange rind
salt and freshly ground black pepper

generous sprig thyme
1 bay leaf
2 fennel stalks
pinch of saffron
1 kg (2 lb) potatoes, cut in pieces
garlic croûtons
finely chopped parsley

1. Clean and scale the sardines.
2. In a large, heavy saucepan, make a bed of onions, tomatoes, garlic, orange rind, and all the herbs except the parsley.
3. Season well with salt and freshly ground black pepper.
4. Place the potatoes on the top.
5. Cover the potatoes generously with water, and cook briskly for 10 to 15 minutes.
6. Add the sardines and continue boiling for a further 5 minutes, or until the potatoes are cooked.
7. Drain off the stock into a soup tureen, and remove the potatoes and sardines to a dish.
8. Serve the liquid and remaining vegetables as a soup, accompanied by garlic croûtons.
9. Serve the sardines and potatoes, sprinkled with chopped parsley, to follow.

Trouffade

Potato hot pot
Many variations of this dish appear all over the Massif Central. This recipe uses a local Cantal cheese called Tomme, which is soft and creamy in texture, but any soft creamy cheese may be substituted. Alternatively a hard cheese such as a local Cheddar or Gruyère, coarsely grated, may be used.

Serves 6

125 g (4 oz) streaky bacon or speck, cut into chunky pieces.
500 g (1 lb) potatoes, thinly sliced

250 g (8 oz) Tomme or alternative cheese, coarsely grated
salt and freshly ground black pepper

1. Heat the bacon or speck in a heavy bottomed frying pan over a moderate heat until the fat runs out.
2. Add the potatoes and cook for 5-6 minutes, turning constantly to brown them on all sides.
3. Stir in the cheese, taking care not to break up the potato slices.
4. Season with salt and pepper.
5. Leave over a gentle heat for 15 minutes until the base is crisp and brown, watching carefully to make sure that it does not catch.
6. Invert on to a warmed serving plate, and serve.

Poulet Doré aux Câpres Quercy

Marinated, fried chicken pieces with capers

Serves 4

2 eggs
½ cup (4 fl oz) milk
1 lemon
salt and freshly ground black pepper
1-1.5 kg (3 lb) chicken, jointed into 8 pieces
dry breadcrumbs

60 g (2 oz) butter
6 tablespoons oil
2 cloves garlic, finely chopped
3 spring onions (scallions) finely chopped
4 tablespoons dry white wine
1 tablespoon capers

1. Beat together the eggs, milk and the juice of the lemon.
2. Season with the salt and the freshly ground black pepper, and leave the chicken pieces to marinate in this mixture for about 3 hours, turning the pieces often.
3. Drain the chicken and roll the pieces in breadcrumbs.
4. Melt the butter and oil in a large, heavy pan.
5. Cook the garlic and the spring onions gently in the butter and oil until soft.
6. Add the chicken pieces and fry them very gently until they are cooked through, and until the juices run clear when pierced with a fork.
7. When they are cooked, arrange the chicken pieces on a warmed serving plate and keep warm.
8. Pour off the excess fat in the pan, and add the wine. Season with salt and pepper.
9. Reduce the sauce a little, scraping the pan to incorporate all the juices.
10. Add the capers and heat through.
11. Pour the sauce over the chicken pieces and serve immediately.

Tourtière de Poulet aux Salsifis

Chicken tart with Salsifis
From the Restaurant La Crémaillère in Brive La Gaillarde.

Serves 4-6

60 g (2 oz) goose fat
1.5 kg (3 lb) chicken, cut into pieces
4 spring onions (scallions) chopped
1 clove garlic, crushed
¼ cup (1 oz) flour
3 cups (24 fl oz) chicken stock

bouquet garni
1 tomato, quartered
300 g (10 oz) salsifis, chopped
   (chopped cucumber may
   be substituted)
puff pastry (see p. 150)

1. In a heavy pan melt the goose fat, and brown the chicken pieces on all sides.
2. Add the spring onions and garlic.
3. Sprinkle with the flour and stir.
4. Moisten with ½ cup of the chicken stock and cook until the sauce thickens.
5. Add the bouquet garni, and the tomato.
6. Cook for 30 minutes on the top of the stove, then allow to cool.
7. Heat the remaining chicken stock to boiling point in a small saucepan.
8. Add the chopped salsifis or cucumber and cook for 5 minutes. Drain well, and add to the chicken mixture.
9. Line a tart dish with puff pastry.
10. Preheat the oven to 180°C (350°F).
11. Fill the tart with the chicken and salsifis or cucumber mixture. Cover the tart with pastry, remembering to leave a small hole for the steam to escape.
12. Bake for 40 minutes or until golden brown.
13. Serve hot.

Épaule d'Agneau à l'Albigeoise

Stuffed and rolled shoulder of lamb with garlic

Serves 4-6

250 g (8 oz) best sausage meat
250 g (8 oz) pigs' liver, minced
2 cloves garlic, crushed
2 tablespoons oil
2 tablespoons parsley, finely chopped
2 sprigs thyme
salt and freshly ground black pepper

1 shoulder of lamb, boned
   and flattened
30 g (1 oz) butter
12 cloves garlic
750 g (1½ lb) medium sized whole
   new potatoes
finely chopped parsley

1. Preheat the oven to 180°C (350°F).
2. Make the stuffing by mixing together the sausage meat, pigs' liver and garlic. Fry in a little of the oil until it is cooked through.
3. Add the chopped parsley and the thyme, and season with salt and freshly ground black pepper. Mix well.
4. Lay out the flattened shoulder of lamb, and spread with the stuffing mixture.
5. Roll the shoulder up and secure with string.
6. Melt the butter and the remaining oil in a flameproof casserole dish and fry the rolled shoulder lightly until it is golden on all sides.
7. Blanch the whole garlic cloves by plunging them into boiling water for 2 minutes.
8. Surround the meat with the potatoes and the blanched garlic cloves. Season the potatoes with a little salt and freshly ground black pepper.
9. Bake the shoulder in the oven for about 1¼ to 1½ hours until the meat is cooked, and the potatoes golden.
10. At the last moment, sprinkle the dish with a little chopped parsley, and serve from the casserole in which it was cooked.

La Crémaillère, Brive-la-Gaillarde

Limousin is famous for its beef, pork, geese and fruit, especially cherries. In one form or another, all of these appear regularly in the frequently changed menu at la Crémaillère. Chef Charles Reynal operates a small but exceptionally efficient kitchen and his dining room enjoys a well deserved popularity. Here I have eaten delicious confit d'oie and a clafoutis made with the largest and most flavoursome cherries I have ever had.

Above: *A selection of dishes from La Crémaillère in Brive-la-Gaillarde.*
Clockwise from bottom left: Black Pudding with Chestnuts, Almond Biscuits (p. 73), Goose Preserve, Chicken Tart with Salsifis, Cherry Clafoutis, Smoked Goose Salad.

Cassoulet de Castelnaudary

Casserole of white beans baked with various meats
The outstanding dish of Languedoc is the cassoulet, cooked slowly for a long time.
Although it is time-consuming to prepare, the cassoulet can be cooked in easy stages,
assembled and refrigerated for a day or so before the final baking.

Serves 8-10

The Beans and Sausage:
16 cups (4 litres) chicken stock
1 kg (2 lb) dry white haricot beans
4 cups (1 litre) water
500 g (1 lb) lean salt pork, in one piece
250 g (8 oz) fresh pork rind (optional)
500 g (1 lb) garlic pork sausage, fresh
  or smoked
3 whole peeled onions
3 cloves garlic, finely chopped
1 teaspoon dried thyme
bouquet garni
salt and freshly ground black pepper
The Pork and Lamb:
250 g (8 oz) pork fat, diced
500 g (1 lb) pork neck, cut in 5 cm
  (2 in) chunks

500 g (1 lb) boned lamb shoulder, cut
  in 5 cm (2 in) chunks
2 onions, finely chopped
2 sticks celery, finely chopped
1 clove garlic, finely chopped
1 cup (8 fl oz) dry white wine
750 g (1½ lb) firm ripe tomatoes,
  peeled, seeded and chopped
  (or substitute 2 cups drained
  tinned tomatoes)
1 bay leaf
salt and freshly ground black pepper

The Topping:
1½ cups (6 oz) fine dry breadcrumbs
½ cup (¾ oz) finely chopped
  fresh parsley

The Beans and Sausage:
1. In a large, heavy saucepan, bring the chicken stock to the boil.
2. Drop the beans in and bring them to the boil, and boil them for two minutes.
3. Remove the saucepan from the heat and let the beans soak for 1 hour.
4. Place the water, salt pork and pork rind in another pan and bring to the boil. Simmer for 15 minutes then drain the meat and set it aside.
5. With a sharp, pointed knife, pierce a few holes in the sausage.
6. Add the sausage, salt pork and rinds to the beans.
7. Bring the beans to the boil over a brisk heat, and skim the top of any scum.
8. When the stock looks fairly clean, add the whole onions, garlic, thyme, bouquet garni, salt and freshly ground black pepper.
9. Reduce the heat and simmer, uncovered, for 45 minutes, adding more stock or water if necessary. Remove the sausage to a plate with tongs.
10. Cook the beans and salt pork for another 30 to 40 minutes or until the beans are tender.
11. Drain, and transfer the salt pork and rinds to the plate with the sausage. Discard the onions and bouquet garni.
12. Strain the stock through a large sieve into a bowl. Skim off the fat and check the seasoning.
13. Set the beans, stock and meats aside in separate containers.

The Pork and Lamb:
14. Preheat the oven to 160°C (325°F).
15. In a heavy frying pan, sauté the diced pork fat until crisp and brown. Remove the dice and set aside.
16. Pour all but 2 or 3 tablespoons of rendered fat into a small bowl.
17. Heat the fat remaining in the pan, and sauté the pork and lamb chunks, a few at a time, until golden brown, adding more pork fat as necessary.
18. Transfer the meat chunks to a heavy casserole dish.
19. Discard all but 3 tablespoons of fat from the frying pan.
20. Add the chopped onions to the pan and cook gently for 5 minutes.
21. Stir in the celery and garlic and cook for 2 minutes, scraping the pan well.
22. Pour in the wine, bring it to a boil and cook over a high heat until it is reduced by half.
23. Scrape the contents of the pan into the casserole.
24. Gently stir the tomatoes, bay leaf, salt and a little pepper into the casserole.
25. Bring the casserole to the boil on top of the stove.
26. Cover the casserole dish and transfer it to the oven and bake for 1 hour, adding a little water or stock if the meat begins to look dry. Transfer the meat to a bowl.
27. Skim the fat from the juices in the casserole.
28. Strain these juices into the bean stock, discarding the vegetables.

To assemble the Cassoulet:

29. Preheat the oven to 180°C (350°F).

30. Peel the sausage and cut it into 6 mm (¼ in) slices.

31. Cut the salt pork and pork rind into 2.5 cm (1 in) squares.

32. In a heavy 24 cup (6 litre) casserole, at least 12.5 cm (5 in) deep, spread a 3 cm deep layer of beans.

33. Arrange half the sausage, pork, pork rind, diced pork fat, braised pork and lamb on top.

34. Cover with another layer of beans, then the rest of the meat, and finally a last layer of beans, with a few slices of sausage on top.

35. Slowly pour in the bean stock until it almost covers the beans. Spread the breadcrumbs on top.

36. Sprinkle the breadcrumbs with 3 or 4 tablespoons of reserved pork fat.

37. Bring the casserole to the boil on top of the stove.

38. Transfer it, uncovered, to the oven for 1¼ hours, or until the crumbs have formed a firm, dark crust.

39. If desired, the first gratin, or crust, can be pushed gently into the cassoulet and the dish baked until a new crust forms.

40. Serve the cassoulet directly from the casserole, sprinkled with parsley.

Oeufs en Cocotte à la Périgourdine

Eggs cooked in cream with chopped truffles
The finest truffles in France are considered to come from Périgord, and any dish described as 'à la Périgourdine', will almost certainly contain them. This simple dish makes an elegant first course.

For each person:

knob of butter
1 tablespoon fresh cream
1 egg

1 small teaspooon chopped truffle
salt and freshly ground black pepper

1. Melt the butter in an individual china ramekin that has a lid.

2. Tilt the ramekin so that the sides are buttered.

3. Spoon in the cream.

4. Carefully break in the egg.

5. Cover with the chopped truffle.

6. Season to taste with salt and freshly ground black pepper. Cover with the lid.

7. Place in a pan of boiling water on top of the stove, and bring it to the boil again.

8. Reduce the heat and simmer very gently for about 8 minutes. Serve very hot.

Canard au Poivre Vert

Duckling with green peppercorns
From the Hôtel D'Étape in Saint-Flour.

Serves 4

2 tablespoons olive oil
100 g (3½ oz) butter
1 duckling — about 2.5 kg (5 lb)
1¼ cups (10 fl oz) demi-glace sauce
  (see p. 149)

½ cup (4 fl oz) cream
1½ tablespoons green peppercorns
salt

1. Preheat the oven to 220°C (425°F).
2. In a heavy casserole dish heat the oil and butter.
3. Brown the duckling on all sides, and cook, uncovered, in the hot oven for ¾ hour.
4. Remove the dish from the oven, and set the duckling aside.
5. Add the demi-glace sauce and the cream to the pan juices, and blend well with a wire whisk.
6. Add the green peppercorns, and blend well. Correct the seasoning.
7. Carve the duckling into serving pieces and return to the casserole dish.
8. Cover the dish, and allow the duckling to simmer in the sauce until tender, (approximately 45 minutes).
9. When the duckling is ready to serve, transfer it to a clean serving dish, and cover with the sauce.
10. The duckling should be accompanied by green vegetables.

Terrine de Campagne

Country style pâté
From the Hôtel D'Étape in Saint-Flour.

Serves 10

2 kg (4 lb) pork neck, with the
  fat removed
1 kg (2 lb) pork liver
1 leek, chopped

1 onion, chopped
salt and freshly ground black pepper
½ cup (4 fl oz) Madeira

1. Preheat the oven to 150°C (300°F).
2. Put all the ingredients except the Madeira through the coarse blade of a food processor or food mill.
3. Add the Madeira and mix well.
4. Butter a terrine dish generously, and fill with the mixture.
5. Cover the terrine dish, stand it in a dish of hot water, and place in the oven.
6. Cook in a slow oven for 4 hours.
7. Allow the terrine to cool thoroughly and set before serving.

Hôtel d'Étape, Saint-Flour.

Hôtel d'Étape is an example of a family-run French country hotel and restaurant. Here the fine products of the region: pork, duck and freshwater crayfish are carefully and skilfully prepared. In addition to the restaurant, Victor Roux and his wife breed ducks, geese and guinea fowl and have a cannery where they preserve a fine range of 'Conserves Maison': foie gras, confit of duck, tripe, civet of rabbit, mushrooms and other local products.

Above: *A selection of dishes from the Hôtel d'Étape in Saint-Flour.*
Clockwise from bottom left: Galantine of pork, Goose liver pâté, Duck with green peppercorns, Crayfish a l'armouricaine.

Côtes de Veau à la Languedocienne

Veal chops with onions, ham and green olives

Serves 6-8

3 tablespoons chicken fat (if
  unavailable substitute butter)
6-8 veal chops
1 large onion, finely chopped
3 tablespoons raw ham, finely diced

salt and freshly ground black pepper
20 green olives, stoned
2 cloves garlic, crushed
4 tablespoons dry white wine

1. In a heavy frying pan, melt the chicken fat.
2. Gently fry the veal chops until they are well browned on both sides.
3. Add the onion, and ham and shake the pan well. Season with salt and pepper.
4. Simmer all these ingredients together until the veal is cooked through.
5. Add the olives and garlic and heat for a few minutes.
6. Remove the chops to a warmed serving dish.
7. Add the wine to the pan, and scrape all the little brown bits in the pan into the sauce.
8. Correct the seasoning and let the sauce reduce a little.
9. Pour the sauce over the veal chops and serve immediately.

Carré de Porc à la Limousine

Roast pork loin served with braised red cabbage with chestnuts

Serves 6-8

60 g (2 oz) softened butter
1 teaspoon thyme
1 bay leaf, crumbled
1 tablespoon French mustard
1 loin of pork (7-8 cutlets) without
  the rind

salt and freshly ground black pepper
1 medium sized red cabbage
4 tablespoon light stock (veal or
  chicken)
4 tablespoons pork fat
20 raw chestnuts, peeled and chopped

1. Preheat the oven to 230°C (450°F).
2. Mix the softened butter, thyme, bay leaf and mustard to a smooth paste and rub well into the pork.
3. Sprinkle to taste with salt and freshly ground black pepper, and leave to stand at room temperature.
4. Arrange the meat, fat side up, in a roasting pan, and brown in the oven for 15 minutes.
5. Reduce the heat to 180°C (350°F) and cook until the meat is done, about 1½ hours.
6. As soon as the pork loin is in the oven, prepare the red cabbage.
7. Shred the cabbage and place it in an earthenware casserole dish.
8. Moisten it with the stock.
9. Add the pork fat and the chestnuts.
10. Season with salt and pepper.
11. Cover the casserole and place it in the oven with the meat to braise gently for 1½ hours.
12. Both the pork loin and the cabbage should be ready at the same time.
13. Arrange the pork loin surrounded by the braised cabbage and chestnuts.
14. Pour over any pan juices and serve.

Clafoutis aux Cerises

Thick cherry pancake, baked in the oven
This is an easily prepared, homely dish from Limousin.

Serves 6

750 g (1½ lb) black cherries, stoned
4 eggs
pinch of salt
½ cup (4 oz) sugar

½ cup (2 oz) flour
60 g (2 oz) butter
1 cup (8 fl oz) milk
caster (powdered) sugar for sprinkling

1. Preheat the oven to 200°C (400°F).
2. Butter a wide shallow ovenproof dish generously.
3. Put the stoned cherries in the dish.
4. Beat the eggs lightly in a bowl.
5. Whisk in the salt and the sugar.
6. Blend in the flour.
7. Melt half of the butter, and beat into the batter.
8. Pour in the milk, beating well.
9. Pour this batter over the cherries.
10. Dot with the remaining butter.
11. Bake for 35-40 minutes, until the batter has set.
12. Sprinkle with sugar and serve either hot or cold, accompanied by whipped cream.

Tuiles aux Noix

Nut biscuits
From the Restaurant La Crémaillère in Brive La Gaillarde.

Makes about 16 biscuits

1½ cups (10 oz) caster (powdered)
sugar
3 tablespoons cornflour (cornstarch)
2 eggs

2 egg whites
6 drops nut essence
¾ cup (3 oz) walnuts, chopped
¾ cup (3 oz) almonds, chopped

1. Preheat the oven to 190°C (375°F).
2. Mix the sugar, cornflour, whole eggs, egg whites and nut essence together.
3. Grease a large baking sheet and dust with flour.
4. Spread large spoonfuls of the mixture onto the baking sheet to form oval shapes.
5. Sprinkle these shapes with the chopped nuts.
6. Cook in the oven for 7-10 minutes.
7. Lift off the sheet with the help of a palette knife, and drape each tuile over a rolling pin to cool in the characteristic curled shape.
8. Repeat until all the biscuit mixture has been used.

Western Pyrenees

(Gascogne, the Basque Country, Béarn, the County of Foix, the Roussillon).

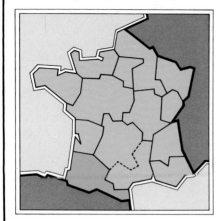

Strong are the characters and determined are the natures of mountain people. The Pyrenees, rough, inaccessible and in parts impenetrable have bred their own type of person. Many, like the Gascons and the Basques are known for their quick temper and determination. Over the centuries most parts have acquired their own regional cuisine. Gascogne, the largest of the regions, is well known for its egg dishes. The confit of goose and the fois gras share their fame with those of Perigord and Alsace. Pommes de Terre à la Landaise, the truly peasant dish reflects the cooking of a poorer countryside. The mountain meadows, though sparse, produce tasty lamb and their milk is made into local cheeses.

In the Armagnac district, renowned for its brandy, many of the dishes are made with the addition of this great spirit, while Bayonne ham is a frequently found ingredient in the cooking of the Basque country.

The Basque cuisine shows both French and Spanish influence and many of its fish dishes are similar to those prepared south of the Pyrenees. Mountain streams yield trout and salmon and the forests teem with game.

Béarn is famous for its Garbure, a heavy stew. Love and care and lots of experience go into the making of it. Despite its peasant character and taste, it is a great dish. Another dish of the Béarn is the more luxurious Poule au Pot, a stuffed chicken boiled in bouillon. It is surprising that a region which raises few pigs should produce such excellent hams as the Jambons de Bayonne, whose fame goes well beyond the confines of this southernmost region of France, and while beef is not plentiful either, Boeuf en Daube à la Béarnaise is a very popular regional dish.

The County of Foix and the Roussillon form two interesting culinary pockets. The former developed its independent character thanks to the number of capable rulers who encouraged and maintained regional differences. Well known for its pork products, especially hams and sausages the region also raises some very good lamb and mutton.

The cuisine of the Roussillon is interesting as it combines both Provençal as well as Catalan influences. Many of its specialities are described as 'à la Catalan' and are characterised by a generous use of garlic so typical in Catalan cooking across the border. Along the shores, fish is the main ingredient of local dishes, most of which are very spicy and again more related to Spanish cooking than to the cuisine of Provence.

The Cathederal of Ste-Cécile on the River Tarn in Albi.

Garbure

Bacon and vegetable soup
A magnificent broth which makes not only a very savoury soup, but also a delicious stew.
Garbure is one of the classic dishes of the Béarn district.

Serves 6-8

500 g (1 lb) white beans, dried
2 bay leaves
2 sprigs thyme
4 sprigs parsley
250 g (8 oz) potatoes, peeled
   and quartered
500 g (1 lb) green beans, cut
1.5 kg (3 lb) confit d'oie (preserved
   goose) or salt pork

freshly ground black pepper
4 tablespoons goose fat or olive oil
2 carrots, thickly sliced
2 turnips, thickly sliced
4 leeks, sliced
1 onion, sliced
2 cups (8 oz) cabbage
   coarsely chopped
croûtons

1. Soak the beans in cold water for several hours.
2. Drain and rinse them.
3. Put the beans into a large flameproof casserole with the bay leaves, thyme and parsley.
4. Add the potatoes, green beans, preserved goose or pork and enough water to cover.
5. Season to taste with pepper, but add very little if any salt as the preserved goose, or salt pork, is highly salted.
6. Cook, covered for 1½ hours, adding more water from time to time if necessary.
7. Heat the goose fat or olive oil in a heavy frying pan, and sauté the carrots, turnips, leeks and onion without letting them take on any colour.
8. Add these vegetables to the soup.
9. Continue cooking at a gentle simmer for another ½ hour.
10. Remove the goose or salt pork, and keep warm.
11. Add the cabbage and continue cooking for a further 45 minutes.
12. The soup, whcih should by now be very thick, is ready to be served, accompanied by croûtons of French bread.
13. The meat is served separately, accompanied by steamed potatoes, and whole baby carrots and turnips which can be added to the soup during the final half hour of cooking.

Piperade

A delicious first course, or light meal of eggs, blended with tomatoes, peppers and ham.

Serves 4-6

30 g (1 oz) butter
4 tablespoons oil
375 g (12 oz) onions, finely sliced
500 g (1 lb) green peppers, cored,
   seeded and coarsely chopped
1 kg (2 lb) tomatoes, peeled, seeded
   and chopped

3 cloves garlic, crushed
bouquet garni
salt and freshly ground black pepper
4-6 thin slices raw ham
8-10 eggs, separated
chopped parsley to garnish

1. Heat the butter and half the oil in a large frying pan.
2. Sauté the onions until they begin to soften.
3. Add the peppers and cook for 2 to 3 minutes.
4. Stir in the tomatoes, garlic, bouquet garni, salt and pepper.
5. Simmer gently for 30 minutes.
6. Fry the ham in the remaining oil until tender. Keep warm.
7. Remove the vegetables from the heat and discard the bouquet garni.
8. Beat the egg whites until stiff.
9. Mix with the egg yolks and add to the cooked vegetable mixture.
10. Stir quickly with a wooden spoon over a moderate heat until the mixture thickens and is blended, with a light and foamy mousse-like consistency.
11. Place the slices of ham on top.
12. Garnish with parsley and serve immediately.

Pommes de Terre à la Landaise

Potatoes à la Landaise

Serves 6

3 tablespoons oil
2 medium onions, finely chopped
185 g (6 oz) raw ham or speck, diced
750 g (1½ lb) potatoes, peeled and cut
  in large dice

salt and freshly ground black pepper
3 cloves garlic, finely chopped
parsley to garnish.

1. Heat the oil in a large frying pan with a lid.
2. Fry the onions and ham until both are well browned.
3. Add the potatoes.
4. Season with salt and pepper.
5. Cook with the lid on for about 20 minutes, stirring from time to time to make sure that the potatoes do not catch and are well blended with the ham and onions.
6. When the potatoes are cooked, add the garlic and mix well.
7. Turn into a warmed vegetable dish and garnish with parsley. Serve.

Côtes de Porc à la Gasconne

Pork chops à la Gasconne

Serves 6

12 cloves garlic
6 pork chops
salt and freshly ground black pepper
1 teaspoon powdered thyme
1 bay leaf
2 tablespoons oil

2 teaspoons vinegar
60 g (2 oz) butter
about 40 black olives, stoned
4 tablespoons dry white wine
4 tablespoons light stock
chopped parsley to garnish

1. Cut one of the garlic cloves into slivers, and insert a couple into each chop, near the bone.
2. Make a marinade by combining salt, pepper, powdered thyme, bay leaf, oil and vinegar.
3. Turn the chops in this mixture and leave to marinate for 1 hour.
4. Melt the butter in a large frying pan with a lid.
5. Fry the drained chops quickly in the butter, just to stiffen them.
6. Peel the remaining cloves of garlic and blanch them by plunging them into boiling water for 2 minutes. Drain well.
7. Add the garlic cloves to the frying pan.
8. Cover the pan and reduce the heat so that the chops simmer gently until they're cooked, about 15 minutes.
9. When they are nearly cooked, add the olives to the pan.
10. Finish cooking, and remove the chops and olives to a warmed serving dish.
11. Dilute the pan juices with the wine, scraping all the little bits from the pan.
12. Add the stock and bring to the boil for a few minutes until it reaches the right consistency.
13. Correct the seasoning, and pour over the chops.
14. Sprinkle with chopped parsley and serve.

Saumon à l'Oseille

Salmon with sorrel sauce
If salmon is unobtainable use a large trout. This recipe comes from the Restaurant Noël in Realmont.

Serves 4

800 g (1 lb 9 oz) salmon, cut into escalopes
2½ cups (20 fl oz) white wine

1 bunch sorrel, finely chopped
1¼ cups (10 fl oz) cream
salt and freshly ground black pepper

1. Poach the escalopes of salmon in the white wine.
2. When they are cooked, remove from the liquid and keep warm.
3. Cook the sorrel in this liquid.
4. When cooked, add the cream and bring to the boil.
5. Check the seasoning.
6. Cover the salmon with this sauce and serve very hot.

Cassoulet Fermier

Farmer's cassoulet
From the Restaurant Noël in Realmont.

Serves 4-6

500 g (1 lb) neck of lamb
200 g (6 oz) belly of pork
100 g (3 oz) pork skin
250 g (8 oz) onions, chopped
2 cloves garlic, chopped
2 tablespoons tomato paste

salt and freshly ground black pepper
2½ cups (1 lb) white haricot beans, soaked overnight
300 g (9 oz) Toulouse garlic sausage
1 cup (4 oz) dry breadcrumbs

1. Preheat the oven to 150°C (300°F).
2. Cut the lamb, pork and pork skin into pieces.
3. Brown the meat in a heavy pan.
4. Add the chopped onions and cook, shaking the pan regularly.
5. Add the garlic, the tomato paste, and enough water to cover the contents of the pan.
6. Season with salt and pepper and cook in a slow oven.
7. Drain the haricot beans, cover with fresh water and simmer until cooked.
8. Grill the sausage, and cut into 5 or 6 pieces.
9. When the meat is three quarters cooked (after about 2¼ hours) add the haricot beans and the sausage.
10. Correct the seasoning.
11. Cover the top of the cassoulet with the breadcrumbs.
12. Return the dish to the oven uncovered for 45 minutes.
13. The cassoulet should have a crust on the top when it is ready to serve.

Hôtel Restaurant Noël, Realmont.
One of the most pleasant aspects of travelling through France is the element of surprise in finding restaurants of exceptional quality in unsuspected places. Off the beaten track in Realmont, just south of Albi, I found just such a surprise. At the Hôtel Noël, Maître Cuisinier Noël Galinier prepares masterful examples of traditional and regional dishes. He is famous for his Cassoulet Fermier, probably the best known of Languedoc specialities. Always enthusiastic about using local products, he prepares Pascade au Roquefort using the fine cheese from Roquefort-sur-Soulzon.

Above: *A selection of dishes from Chez Noël in Realmont. Clockwise from bottom left: Roquefort Crêpes, Farmer's Cassoulet, Crayfish Flambées, Duck Liver Terrine, Salmon with Sorrel, Tournedos with morilles, Trout in Cream.*

Sauté d'Agneau à la Navarraise

Lamb sautéed with sweet red peppers, garlic, paprika and cayenne pepper
A recipe that is typical of the south-west region of France.

Serves 6

1 leg of lamb, boned and cut in 2.5 cm
   (1 in) cubes
salt and freshly ground black pepper
60 g (2 oz) unsalted butter
5 tablespoons oil
2 onions, peeled and thinly sliced

1 tablespoon vinegar
6 sweet red peppers, seeded and diced
1 clove garlic, crushed
1 teaspoon paprika
dash of powdered cayenne pepper, or
   1 small hot pimento

1. Season the lamb cubes with salt and pepper.
2. Heat the butter and 2 tablespoons of the oil in a heavy frying pan.
3. Sauté the pieces of lamb until they are golden brown at the edges.
4. Add the onions, cover the pan and cook for 5 minutes, stirring from time to time.
5. Add the vinegar, stir, and leave covered, off the heat.
6. Heat the remaining oil in another frying pan.
7. Sauté the red peppers gently, stirring often.
8. Stir in the garlic and paprika and cook gently for 7 to 8 minutes.
9. Add the peppers to the meat.
10. Add the cayenne pepper.
11. Taste, and correct the seasoning.
12. Simmer very gently for about 5 minutes.
13. Arrange the sautéed lamb on a warmed serving dish, sprinkle with the parsley and serve.

Rognons de Veau Gasconne

Kidneys cut in small pieces, flamed in Armagnac and served in a spring onion and
mustard sauce

Serves 6

3-4 veal kidneys
salt and freshly ground black pepper
90 g (3 oz) butter
4 tablespoons oil
125 g (4 oz) button mushrooms
squeeze of lemon juice

½ cup (4 fl oz) Armagnac
1 tablespoon finely chopped spring
   onion (scallion)
½ cup (4 fl oz) dry white wine
½ cup (4 fl oz) cream
1 tablespoon strong French mustard

1. Remove any fat from the kidneys and chop into cubes.
2. Grind a little pepper over them, but not salt as this will make them tough during cooking.
3. Melt half the butter in a small frying pan and add 1 tablespoon of oil.
4. Gently cook the mushrooms for a few minutes, without letting them brown.
5. Season them with salt and pepper and a squeeze of lemon.
6. Heat the rest of the oil in a separate frying pan, and quickly sauté the kidneys for 3 to 4 minutes.
7. Drain off the oil, pour in the Armagnac and ignite.
8. When the flame has died out, remove the kidneys from the pan and keep warm.
9. Add the rest of the butter to the pan, and the spring onion.
10. Cook for 1 minute.
11. Pour in the wine, bring to the boil and let it reduce over a high heat for 2 minutes.
12. Remove the pan from the heat and add the cream and mustard.
13. Return the pan to the heat to thicken.
14. Add the mushrooms and their cooking liquid.
15. When the sauce has warmed through, put the kidneys in to reheat.
16. Adjust the seasoning if necessary.
17. Arrange the kidneys on a serving dish and cover with the sauce.

Daube de Boeuf à la Béarnaise

Braised beef à la Béarnaise

Serves 6-8

2 kg (4 lb) lean beef, cut in 2.5 cm
  (1 in) cubes
2 onions, sliced
2 carrots, sliced
1 bouquet garni
salt and freshly ground black pepper
1¼ cups (10 fl oz) red wine

4 tablespoons brandy
4 tablespoons oil
250 g (8 oz) bacon, diced
1 large onion, cut in quarters
4 cloves garlic, chopped
1¼ cups (10 fl oz) beef stock or
  hot water
3 tablespoons flour mixed with 1
  tablespoon water for paste.

1. Place the meat in a large bowl, or earthenware casserole with the onions, carrots, bouquet garni, salt and freshly ground black pepper.
2. Add the red wine and brandy and marinate for 5 to 6 hours, stirring occasionally.
3. Preheat the oven to 120°C (250°F).
4. Heat the oil in a frying pan and cook the diced bacon for a few minutes.
5. Add the onion and brown.
6. Drain the meat and reserve the marinade.
7. Sauté the meat with the bacon bits and the onion, until browned, shaking the pan from time to time.
8. Add the garlic and transfer to a casserole dish.
9. In a small saucepan, heat the marinade and allow it to reduce to half the original quantity over a brisk heat.
10. Add the marinade to the meat, and then pour over the hot stock.
11. Make a paste with the flour and water.
12. Spread this paste around the rim of the casserole dish and press the lid down on top to make an air-tight seal. Alternatively, cover the top of the casserole dish with a sheet of greaseproof paper, and then place the lid on top.
13. Transfer the casserole dish to the preheated oven, and cook very slowly for 3 to 4 hours.
14. When ready to serve, remove the dish from the oven.
15. Skim the fat from the surface and correct the seasoning.
16. Serve straight from the dish.

Ballotines d'Agneau

Ballotines of lamb

Serves 6-8

750 g (1½ lb) minced lamb
2 medium onions, finely chopped
2 cloves garlic, crushed
1½ tablespoons parsley,
  finely chopped

1½ teaspoons thyme
3 eggs, separated
flour
1½ cups (6 oz) dried breadcrumbs
oil

1. Mix the meat with the finely chopped onions, garlic and herbs.
2. Add the egg yolks to the meat mixture and blend well.
3. Make the meat into small ball shapes and dust with flour.
4. Beat the egg whites until they are stiff and white.
5. Coat the meat balls with the egg white.
6. Then coat them in breadcrumbs.
7. In a large frying pan pour in oil to a depth of 1 cm (½ in) and heat it to sizzling point.
8. Gently fry the meat balls in the hot oil, turning regularly so that they become cooked on all sides and golden in colour.
9. Drain and serve.

Aubergine au Gratin à la Catalan

Eggplant au gratin à la Catalan

Serves 6

3 eggplants (allow one half per person)
salt
4 tablespoons oil
2 onions, finely chopped
3 hard-boiled eggs, chopped

3 tablespoons fresh breadcrumbs
1 tablespoon parsley, finely chopped
2 cloves garlic, crushed
salt and freshly ground black pepper
butter

1. Cut the eggplants in half lengthways.
2. Make a few shallow incisions in the pulp, sprinkle with salt and leave in a dish to 'sweat' for 1 hour.
3. Heat the oil in a heavy frying pan.
4. Pat the egg plants dry and fry in the oil, turning from time to time, until the centres are soft.
5. Drain and allow to cool a little.
6. Carefully scoop out the pulp without damaging the outside skin.
7. Fry the onions gently in the oil remaining in the pan until they are cooked through.
8. Mix the chopped eggplant pulp with the onions, hard-boiled eggs, breadcrumbs, parsley and garlic.
9. Season to taste with salt and freshly ground black pepper, and mix well.
10. Fill the eggplant halves with this mixture, and put into a buttered, overproof dish.
11. Sprinkle with a few breadcrumbs and dot with butter.
12. Brown the top of the eggplants under the grill, and serve.

Poulet Sauté à la Basquaise

Fried chicken with onions, peppers and tomatoes

Serves 4

1 chicken, about 1.5 kg (3 lb),
 quartered
salt and freshly ground black pepper
flour
6-7 tablespoons oil
4 onions, thinly sliced
4 red peppers, finely chopped
4 cloves garlic, crushed
10 tomatoes, skinned, seeded
 and chopped

2 tablespoons tomato paste
2 teaspoons sugar
1 bouquet garni
small ham bone or piece of ham
 weighing about 200 g (7 oz)
pinch cayenne pepper
½ cup (4 fl oz) water
1 tablespoon parsley, finely chopped

1. Dust the chicken pieces with salt and flour.
2. Heat 4 tablespoons of oil in a heavy frying pan until sizzling.
3. Sauté the chicken pieces over a high heat until they are lightly browned all over.
4. Reduce the heat, cover the pan and leave to simmer for 10 minutes.
5. Remove the chicken pieces.
6. Add 2 tablespoons of oil to the pan, and cook the onions for 3 minutes, until just coloured.
7. Add another tablespoon of oil if necessary, and put in the peppers.
8. Add the garlic, tomatoes, tomato paste, sugar, bouquet garni and ham.
9. Season to taste with salt, freshly ground black pepper and cayenne pepper.
10. Moisten with the water, adding a little more if necessary.
11. Cover, and cook the sauce for 15 minutes.
12. Return the chicken to the pan, cover and leave to simmer over a gentle heat for about 30 minutes, or until the chicken is tender.
13. Serve in a deep serving dish, sprinkled with finely chopped parsley, and accompanied by a rice pilaf.

La Poule au Pot du Béarnais

Stuffed boiled chicken with vinaigrette and egg sauce
This is one of the favourite family dishes of this part of France, which makes both a soup and meat dish in one.

Serves 4-6

90 g (3 oz) chicken livers
3 tablespoons fresh breadcrumbs
3 tablespoons milk
125 g (4 oz) sausage meat
1 tablespoon finely chopped parsley
salt and freshly ground black pepper
1 egg
1 good fat boiling chicken, about
  2 kg (4 lb)
90 g (3 oz) butter
4 carrots, chopped
2 turnips, chopped
1 onion, chopped
1 leek, sliced
1 stalk celery
fresh vegetables in season

Sauce vinaigrette a l'oeuf:
1 small spring onion (scallion),
  finely chopped
1 tablespoon finely chopped parsley
salt and freshly ground black pepper
3 tablespoons olive oil
2 teaspoons lemon juice
chives, chopped, if available
1 egg

1. Pound the chicken livers until broken up.
2. Soak the breadcrumbs in the milk, and squeeze them dry.
3. Mix together the pounded liver, breadcrumbs, sausage meat, parsley and seasoning.
4. Blend this mixture together with an egg.
5. Stuff the chicken, and secure the opening by tying up or sewing with fine thread.
6. Take a large deep saucepan or earthenware pot, making sure that there is plenty of room for a variety of vegetables as well as the chicken and plenty of water.
7. Melt the butter in this saucepan, and brown the chicken all over.
8. Add the carrots, turnips, onion, leek, celery, salt and pepper, and pour in boiling water to cover the contents of the pan.
9. Bring the water to the boil again and remove any scum which comes to the surface of the pan.
10. Cover the pan and reduce the heat so that the water simmers very gently.
11. Cook for 2¼ hours.
12. Remove the vegetables which by now are rather sodden and tasteless, and replace with fresh vegetables in season, such as baby carrots, peas, zucchinis (courgettes) etc.
13. Continue cooking for a further 40 minutes, or less, depending on the vegetables which have been added.
14. Remove the chicken from the soup and drain.
15. Serve the chicken with the vegetables all round, and a sauce vinaigrette a l'oeuf served separately.
16. A little pasta can be added to the broth and cooked for a few minutes before being served as a first course, or it can be kept for another meal.

Sauce vinaigrette a l'oeuf:
1. Mix together the spring onion, parsley, salt and freshly ground black pepper.
2. Add the olive oil, lemon juice and if available, a few chives, chopped with scissors.
3. Boil an egg for 3 minutes.
4. Scoop out the yolk and add to the olive oil and lemon mixture. Stir well.
5. Chop the egg white and add to the sauce, and serve.

Crème Chaude aux Pruneaux

Prune cream

Serves 6

1¼ cups (8 oz) prunes	**2 eggs**
weak cold tea	**1¼ cups (10 fl oz) milk**
1½ cups (6 oz) flour	**75 g (2½ oz) butter**
¼ cup (2 oz) sugar	**vanilla essence**
pinch of salt	**1 tablespoon rum**

1. Soak the prunes in weak tea for several hours, or overnight if possible.
2. Drain them and remove the stones.
3. Preheat the oven to 200°C (400°F).
4. Mix the flour, salt and sugar in a mixing bowl.
5. Add the eggs and then the milk to make a thick batter.
6. Melt the butter.
7. Whip the butter into the batter mixture.
8. Add the vanilla and the rum.
9. Butter an ovenproof tart dish and arrange the prunes in it.
10. Pour the batter mixture over the prunes.
11. Bake for 35 minutes, or until the cream is set.
12. Turn out while still warm and serve with whipped cream.

Gâteau aux Amandes

Almond cake
This may be served for afternoon tea or as a dessert to accompany vanilla ice cream or chocolate cream.

1 cake, about 22 cm (9 in) in diameter, for 10-12 people.

20 very fresh egg whites	**3¼ cups (13 oz) flour**
pinch of salt	**a few drops lemon essence, or the**
3¾ cups (24 oz) caster (powdered)	**finely grated rind of 1 lemon**
sugar	**½ cup (2 oz) slivered almonds**
250 g (8 oz) unsalted butter, softened	

1. Preheat the oven to 190°C (385°F).
2. Beat the egg whites until stiff with a good pinch of salt.
3. Carefully add the sugar, bit by bit, whisking constantly. (The mixture will change consistency, becoming creamier, but firm.)
4. Add, all together, the well softened butter, the sifted flour and the lemon essence or rind.
5. Mix carefully so that the egg whites remain stiff.
6. Pour the mixture into a well buttered cake tin, 22 cm, (9 in) in diameter.
7. Sprinkle the top generously with almonds.
8. Bake for about 45 minutes.
9. Test with the point of a trussing needle to see whether it is cooked. The needle should come out damp but clean.
10. Turn out the cake and allow to become cold before slicing.

Gâteau Basque

Basque cake

1 — 22 cm (9 in) tart

Pastry:
30 g (1 oz) fresh bakers' yeast
125 g (4 oz) butter
2 cups (8 oz) flour
⅔ cup (5 oz) sugar
2 eggs

Filling:
½ cup (4 oz) sugar
1 tablespoon flour
3 tablespoons cornflour (cornstarch)
1¼ cups (10 fl oz) milk
pinch of salt
2 egg yolks
a little jam to brush over the top

1. Preheat the oven to 180°C (350°F).
2. Dissolve the yeast in a little warm water.
3. Make the pastry by rubbing the butter into the flour and sugar.
4. Bind together with the eggs and the yeast.
5. Knead the pastry for about 5 minutes to make sure that the yeast is evenly distributed throughout the pastry.
6. For the filling, mix the sugar, flour and cornflour in a saucepan with a little milk to make a paste. Add the salt.
7. Bring the rest of the milk to the boil, and add it to the paste, whisking well all the time.
8. Whisking continuously, add the egg yolks.
9. Return the saucepan to the heat and cook for a few minutes, whisking all the time.
10. Pour in a bowl and leave to cool.
11. Divide the pastry in two, and roll out one half thinly.
12. Line a tart tin with the pastry.
13. Pour the cream filling on top of the pastry, and top with the rest of the pastry.
14. Cook in the preheated oven for 20 minutes.
15. Brush the top with a little jam and cook for a further 5 minutes.
16. Serve hot.

Nougat

Candy made with roasted almonds and honey

Makes approximately 30 squares

⅔ cup (8 oz) honey
1 cup (8 oz) sugar
1 tablespoon orange blossom water or
½ teaspoon orange extract

1 egg white, stiffly beaten
500 g (1 lb) almonds, blanched,
chopped and heated in the oven

1. Cook together the honey and the sugar to the small crack degree, 125°C (269°F).
2. Add the orange blossom water or orange extract and the egg white.
3. Melt over a gentle flame, stirring constantly, and bring the mixture to the broil degree 119°C (246°F).
4. Add the almonds.
5. Pour this mixture in a flat baking tin which has been lined with sheets of rice-paper.
6. Cover with sheets of the same paper.
7. Place a wooden board on top of the nougat with a heavy weight on the top of it.
8. Leave until the nougat is lukewarm.
9. Cut the nougat into squares or shapes.

Bordeaux

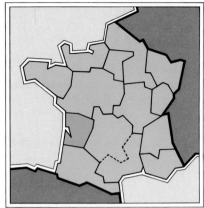

If great wines create a great cuisine, the Bordeaux region should have the best food in France. The names of its wines are the most famous in the world: Château d'Yquem, Haut-Brion, Lafit-Rothschild, Margaux and Latour to mention only a few of many.

It is interesting to note that as the range of wines extends from the aristrocratic grand premier cru and grands crus through the first, second and third growth wines to the crus bourgeois, artisans and paysans, so does the range of Bordeaux cooking. Such classical dishes of the Bordelaise repertoire as Entrecôte or Écrevisses à la Bordelaise or Foie Gras with Grapes are a great complement to the best of the Bordeaux wines, while the more simple sausages with oysters is matched well when washed down with a humble but still pleasant bourgeois.

The cooking term 'à la bordelaise' denotes several ways of preparing the food. It may mean cooked in a sauce bordelaise, which consists of red wine, butter, tomato purée, shallots, thyme, nutmeg and bone marrow. It may also mean that a mirepoix of vegetables has been used, as for example in the Écrevisses à la Bordelaise. It also means that the dish is accompanied by mushrooms à la bordelaise or by artichokes and potatoes.

As if it is not enough that Bordeaux produces the best wines in France and therefore in the world, it also produces the world's best brandy: the Cognac. Aged in limousin oak, its quality depends on the use of particular grape varieties and the careful ageing in wood, the ageing process being halted once it is bottled. The uses of Cognac in cooking are many, and its flavour adds a particular character that no other brandy can give. After Paris and Lyon, Bordeaux well deserves the title of one of the country's gastronomic centres. Its standing as an important trading port and commercial centre has over the ages attracted great wealth which has resulted in a patronage of gourmet establishments of the highest order.

At its best, Bordeaux cooking is Haute-Cuisine, the products of years of great culinary refinement well justified by the presence of the greatest wines in France.

The Dordogne Valley.

Tourin

Onion soup from Bordeaux

Serves 6-8

60 g (2 oz) pork dripping or fat
750 g (1½ lb) onions, finely sliced
7½ cups (2 litres) light veal or
 chicken stock

salt and freshly ground black pepper
2 cloves garlic, crushed
4 egg yolks
6-8 rounds of French bread

1. Melt the pork fat in a large, heavy saucepan, and gently fry the onions until they are soft and just beginning to turn brown.
2. Add the stock, bring to the boil and simmer for 15 to 20 minutes.
3. Season with salt, freshly ground pepper and the crushed garlic.
4. Mix the egg yolks together in a large bowl.
5. Slowly whisk in the hot soup, a little at a time.
6. The mixture will thicken as the eggs cook.
7. Return the thickened soup to the saucepan, and stir over a gentle heat for five minutes.
8. Take great care not to let the soup boil.
9. Serve with rounds of bread roasted in the oven in a baking dish with a few drops of oil.

Moules à la Bordelaise

Mussels à la Bordelaise

Serves 6

2 kg (4 lb) mussels, trimmed, scraped
 and washed
½ cup (4 fl oz) dry white wine
1 onion, sliced
parsley
thyme
bayleaf

The Mirepoix:
125 g (4 oz) butter
2 small carrots, finely sliced
1 large onion, finely chopped
1 stalk of celery, finely chopped
sprig of thyme
¾ cup (6 fl oz) fish velouté sauce
 (see p. 147)
1 cup (8 fl oz) fresh cream
1 tablespoon tomato paste
lemon juice
salt and pepper
finely chopped parsley

1. Place the cleaned mussels in a large saucepan, together with the wine, onion, parsley, thyme and bay leaf.
2. Cook over a high heat for 5 minutes or until all the mussels have opened.
3. Drain the mussels, reserving the liquid.
4. Remove and discard one shell from each mussel, place the mussels in a deep bowl and keep them hot.
5. To make the mirepoix, melt half the butter in a heavy saucepan and cook the vegetables, covered, over a gentle heat until they are very tender.
6. Add the fish velouté sauce to the mirepoix.
7. Strain the mussel stock into the mirepoix.
8. Add the cream and tomato paste and blend well.
9. Bring this sauce to the boil and whisk in the remaining butter and a squeeze of lemon juice.
10. Correct the seasoning.
11. Pour this sauce, boiling hot, over the mussels.
12. Serve sprinkled with chopped parsley.

Foie de Caneton, Sauce à la Dacquoise

Fresh duck livers, served with grape sauce
The proximity to the great vineyards means that there are many Bordeaux recipes which include grapes. This sauce is equally delicious with chicken livers.

Serves 6-8

1 kg (2 lb) ducks' livers, or alternative
90 g (3 oz) butter
1 small onion, chopped
125 g (4 oz) grapes
60 g (2 oz) raisins
125 g (4 oz) ham, chopped

bouquet garni
½ cup (4 fl oz) dry white wine
¼ cup (2 fl oz) chicken stock
flour
1 tablespoon Madeira

1. Since the livers take only a few minutes to cook it is wise to prepare the sauce before cooking them.
2. Melt 1 tablespoon of the butter in a heavy saucepan and gently cook the onion until it is soft.
3. Add the grapes, raisins, ham, bouquet garni and white wine.
4. Cook until the liquid has reduced to half its volume.
5. Add the chicken stock, correct the seasoning and simmer for 15 minutes.
6. Dry the livers and slice into thin strips.
7. Flour them lightly.
8. Melt the rest of the butter and fry the livers, turning them often, until they are cooked through.
9. Arrange the livers on a serving dish.
10. Add the Madeira to the sauce, pour over the livers and serve.

Ficelles de Brantome Bordelaise

Savoury stuffed pancakes

Serves 8

8 pancakes (see recipe p. 150)
30 g (1 oz) butter
250 g (8 oz) cèpes or other
 mushrooms, sliced

squeeze of lemon
8 thin slices cooked ham
1 cup (8 fl oz) cream
¾ cup (3 oz) grated cheese

1. Make the pancakes and keep them warm.
2. Melt the butter and lightly cook the cèpes or mushrooms for 2 or 3 minutes. Squeeze lemon juice over them.
3. Place a slice of ham on each pancake.
4. Top the ham with the mushrooms.
5. Roll up the pancakes and arrange on an ovenproof serving dish.
6. Whip the cream lightly and spoon over the pancakes.
7. Sprinkle with finely grated cheese, and place under a preheated grill until lightly browned and bubbling.
8. Serve at once.

Le Ris de Veau Braisé au Sauternes

Braised Sweetbreads with Sauternes
This recipe comes from Le Chapon Fin in Bordeaux.

Serves 6

500 g (1 lb) carrots
185 g (6 oz) onions
1 celery root
250 g (8 oz) field mushrooms
⅓ cup (2½ fl oz) olive oil
1 bouquet garni of fresh herbs
   and parsley
1 clove garlic cut in half
6 sweetbreads
2 cups (16 fl oz) sauternes style wine
3 cups (24 fl oz) veal stock (p. 148)

Sauce:
1 cup (8 fl oz) fresh cream

1 tablespoon mousse of foie gras
   (goose liver pâté)
1 tablespoon truffle juice (optional)
pepper
salt

Garnish:
2 tablespoons butter
90 g (3 oz) celery, cut into
   julienne strips
90 g (3 oz) button mushrooms cut into
   julienne strips
185 g (6 oz) carrots cut into
   julienne strips

1. Finely chop the carrots, onions, celery and mushrooms to prepare the mirepoix.
2. Heat the oil in a saucepan and lightly brown the mirepoix. Add the bouquet garni and garlic.
3. Place the sweetbreads on top of the mirepoix and add the sauternes and veal stock. Cover and braise on a low flame for 20-25 minutes.
4. Remove the sweetbreads, place them in a colander and rinse them under cold running water. With a sharp knife remove all skins from the sweetbreads, cut them into slices and keep hot.
5. Strain the cooking juices into a saucepan and cook until reduced by half, add the cream, pâté and truffle juice. Season to taste.
6. To prepare the garnish, lightly sauté the vegetables in the butter. Season.
7. To serve, arrange the slices of sweetbreads on the vegetables and pour the sauce over them.

Pigeonneau de Madame Raymonde

Roast Pigeon Madame Raymonde
From the Restaurant Le Chapon Fin in Bordeaux.

Serves 6

6 pigeons + their livers
60 g (2 oz) foie gras
butter
400 g (12 oz) mushrooms, finely
   chopped and sautéed in butter
50 g (2 oz) beans cooked and
   finely chopped

50 g (2 oz) truffles (optional)
50 g (2 oz) asparagus tips, cooked
salt and freshly ground black pepper
¼ cup (2 fl oz) brandy
¼ cup (2 fl oz) vermouth
300 g (9 oz) butter

1. Preheat the oven to 180°C (350°F).
2. Bone the pigeons, cutting down the backbone, and leaving the skin as intact as possible, in order to make a pocket for the stuffing.
3. Sauté the pigeon livers with the foie gras in a little butter. Mash them with a fork.
4. Make a stuffing by combining the mushrooms, beans, truffles, asparagus tips, liver mixture and salt and pepper to taste.
5. Stuff the pigeons with this mixture, and sew up the opening securely with twine.
6. Place the pigeons in the oven with a little butter on the top and roast for 30-40 minutes, or until cooked.
7. Remove the pigeons from the dish and keep warm.
8. Degrease the pan with the brandy and vermouth, scraping well to incorporate all the pieces of pigeon left in the pan.
9. Allow the sauce to reduce a little, and beat in the butter slowly with a wire whisk.
10. Correct the seasoning and strain the sauce.
11. Arrange the pigeons on a serving dish, garnish with carrots and asparagus tips if desired, and serve with the sauce.

Le Chapon Fin, Bordeaux.

*The Chapon Fin has maintained its flamboyant
'fin de siècle' interior and could quite easily
serve as a backdrop to 'Hello Dolly'
The restaurant has a great past and with its
three stars in the 1930s was among the
best-known establishments in France.
Today, Chef Jean Ramet serves an impressive
array of unusual dishes, many of them in the
best of Bordeaux style.*

Above: *A selection of dishes from Le Chapon
Fin in Bordeaux. Clockwise from bottom left:
Pears with Raspberry Sauce, Roast Pigeon,
Goats' Cheese, Roast Duckling, Sweetbreads in
Sauternes, Salmon with Dill, Chocolate Mousse,
Fruit Loaf with Raspberry Sauce, (p. 93)
Braised Crayfish.* **Right**: *Interior of
Le Chapon Fin.*

Les Écrevisses à la Bordelaise

Crayfish in white wine sauce
King prawns may be substituted where the small European type of crayfish
is unobtainable.

Serves 6

30 raw crayfish or king prawns
5 tablespoons oil
185 g (6 oz) butter
2 tablespoons brandy
2 small carrots, finely chopped
1 large onion, finely chopped
1 stalk of celery, finely chopped
1 bay leaf
sprig of thyme
2 sprigs of parsley

salt and freshly ground black pepper
1 cup (8 fl oz) white wine fish fumet
  (see p. 149)
1⅓ cup (11 fl oz) dry white (Bordeaux)
  wine
1 medium tomato, peeled, seeded
  and chopped
large pinch of tarragon
pinch of cayenne pepper

1. Gut the crayfish or prawns.
2. Heat the oil and half the butter in a large, heavy frying pan and sauté the crayfish or prawns over a fairly high heat until the shells turn red.
3. Shell the crayfish and return them to the pan.
4. Warm the brandy, pour it over the crayfish and ignite it.
5. Add the carrots, onion, celery, bay leaf, thyme, parsley, salt and pepper to taste, and cook for a few minutes over a gentle heat until the onion is tender but not browned.
6. Add the fish fumet, wine, tomato, tarragon and cayenne and gently simmer for 10 minutes.
7. Remove the crayfish and keep them warm.
8. Raise the heat under the sauce and cook it, stirring all the time, until it is quite thick.
9. Beat in the rest of the butter with a wire whisk.
10. Pour the sauce over the crayfish and serve.

Gigot D'Agneau Persillé

Parslied leg of lamb

Serves 6

1 leg of lamb, about 2.5 kg (5 lb)
1 clove garlic, slivered
sprigs of thyme

2 tablespoons finely chopped parsley
3 tablespoons fresh breadcrumbs

1. Preheat the oven to 200°C (400°F).
2. Trim off any excess fat from the lamb.
3. Insert slivers of garlic and small sprigs of thyme into slits in the lamb.
4. Roast the leg of lamb in the preheated oven for about 1 hour, with a little water in the roasting pan to prevent it from catching.
5. Mix the parsley with the breadcrumbs in a bowl.
6. About 10 to 15 minutes before the leg is cooked, coat the leg with the breadcrumb and parsley mixture, taking care to press the mixture well into the fatty surface of the meat so that it adheres.
7. Return the meat to the oven and roast until the surface turns to a golden crust.
8. Arrange on a serving dish, garnished with watercress and lemon quarters.

Cèpes à la Bordelaise

Mushrooms with breadcrumbs and spring onions

Serves 6

500 g (1 lb) button mushrooms
90 g (3 oz) butter
juice of half a lemon
2 tablespoons oil
1 tablespoon chopped spring onions
  (scallions)

2 heaped tablespoons fresh
  breadcrumbs
1 clove garlic, finely chopped
1 tablespoon finely chopped parsley

1. Trim and wash the mushroom caps, reserving the stalks.
2. Melt the butter with the lemon juice in a heavy pan and simmer the mushroom caps for a few minutes. Drain them.
3. Heat the oil in a clean pan and sauté the mushrooms, until they brown slightly.
4. Chop up the mushroom stalks and combine with the spring onions, breadcrumbs, garlic and parsley.
5. Add this combination to the mushrooms and cook for five minutes, stirring regularly.
6. Arrange the mushrooms on a dish, sprinkle with a little lemon juice and chopped parsley and serve.

Le Pain de Fruits au Coulis de Framboises

Fruit loaf with raspberry sauce
From the Restaurant Le Chapon Fin in Bordeaux.

Serves 10

4 egg yolks
½ cup (4 oz) caster (powdered) sugar
1¼ cups (10 fl oz) milk
1 teaspoon vanilla essence
2 teaspoons gelatine
1¼ cups (10 fl oz) cream
125 g (4 oz) strawberries
125 g (4 oz) blackberries
4 peaches, peeled, halved and stoned

Sauce:
125 g (4 oz) raspberries
¾ cup (6 oz) caster (powdered) sugar

1. Beat the egg yolks and the sugar together until they are fluffy.
2. Heat the milk and the vanilla essence.
3. Beating constantly, pour the hot milk on to the egg and sugar mixture, and cook in a double saucepan until the custard thickens a little.
4. Soften the gelatine in a little milk and beat into the custard until dissolved.
5. Strain the custard and allow to cool to room temperature.
6. The custard should be cold, but not set.
7. Whip the cream until it is firm.
8. Gently blend the whipped cream into the custard.
9. Add the whole strawberries, blackberries, and peach halves.
10. Take great care not to crush the fruit while mixing them into the custard.
11. Pour this mixture into a galantine mould, or bread tin.
12. Transfer to the refrigerator for 2 to 3 hours.

Sauce:
1. Blend the raspberries and the caster sugar in a food processor, or food mill.
2. To serve, unmould the 'loaf' and cut in slices.
3. Surround each slice with the raspberry sauce and serve.

The Loire Valley
(Touraine, Anjou, Orléanais, Poitou, Berry)

Touraine shares with the Île-de-France the distinction that its regional dishes have become the basis of a great part of what today is called Haute Cuisine. Nevertheless many of the local dishes show bourgeois simplicity. Renowned for its charcuteries, it produces sausages, pâtés, galantines and the famous Rillettes de Tours. But probably its greatest pride is its roasts. Many of the restaurants of Tours have made their name by offering some of the best roasts in France. Vouvray is the most well-known of Touraine wines, sometimes naturally sparkling, it is light, has a low alcoholic content, is highly flavoured and slightly musky. Not a great wine, but ideal with the many fish dishes of the region.

The history of Anjou is closely linked with that of Touraine and gastronomically shares many of its dishes. Its cuisine is softer, blander and milder than that of the Touraine and like that of its neighbours, it is of peasant origin. Larousse says of the Anjou: 'A land of sweetness and harmony where the cuisine and wines match the nature'. The wines of Anjou are the light whites of Saumur, the rosé of Anjou and Muscadet, the fruity white wine that goes so well with the famous Pike au Beurre Blanc. Pork is delicate and like the surrounding regions, Anjou prides itself on it rillettes, potted pork mince, sausages and black puddings.

The Orléanais is historic country, linked inseparably to the history of France. Here are some of the most famous royal châteaux: Chambard, originally a royal hunting lodge, Blois and many others which reflect their features in the waters of the Loire. Even today the Loire and its tributaries supplies some of the best fish in France. Most of these rivers and in parts even the Loire itself are unpolluted and abound with fresh water crayfish, pike, mullet, shad, bream, eel, carp and of course the noble Loire Salmon. The traditional way of preparing the fish is in "matelot", meaning as a fish stew made with white or red wine, however Salmon and Carp Chambord are two classical and aristocratic dishes which were created in the region.

Poitou, the western-most area of this group of regions is best known for its peasant dishes. High quality cattle, lamb and pigs produce fine meats and the local dishes use these ingredients skilfully. Extensive poultry farming produces chickens, turkeys, guinea fowl and even ducks which are used in the local version of the Confit de Canard, while their livers go to make such dishes as Civray pâté de Foie Gras. In the coastal areas shellfish, Portuguese oysters, mussels and crayfish enrich the table, while the marshes teem with eel and frogs.

The last of the regions is the Berry district to the south of the Touraine and the Orléanais. It is credited with breeding the best sheep in France. Potatoes are popular and they say that soups are eaten 3 times a day! No wonder that the main characteristic of the Berry cuisine is 'agreeable simplicity' and 'rustic quality'.

Château Azay-le-Rideau.

Beurre Blanc
White butter sauce
In the Touraine this is customarily served as a delicate accompaniment to poached fish.

Approximately 1 cup (8 fl oz)

1 spring onion (scallion), finely chopped
salt
pepper
2 tablespoons water

1 tablespoon finest white wine vinegar
150-200 g (5-7 oz) butter, cut into small pieces
finely chopped parsley

1. Put the spring onion in a saucepan with a pinch of salt and pepper. Add the water and vinegar.
2. Boil these ingredients until the liquid is reduced by two thirds. Strain and return the liquid to the pan.
3. Remove the pan to the edge of the stove, and, little by little, stirring all the time, add the butter until it is all absorbed, and the sauce has a creamy appearance.
4. Keep the sauce hot without allowing it to boil.
5. Just before serving, sprinkle with parsley.

Cotriade
This is a kind of bouillabaisse, a true fisherman's meal, which depending on the types of fish used, can be quite economical to prepare.

Serves 6

2 kg (4 lb) fish, such as sardine, mackerel, bream, mullet, eel, etc.
1 kg (2 lb) potatoes, peeled
¾ cup (3 oz) flour
90 g (3 oz) butter
6 slices stale white bread, crusts removed
1 cut clove garlic
salt

Fumet:
1 onion, finely chopped
1 leek, finely chopped
1 clove garlic, crushed
1 bulb fennel, sliced
3 stalks celery, chopped
parsley
1 cup (8 fl oz) dry white wine
4 cups (1 litre) water
salt and pepper

1. Clean the fish, removing the heads and tails.
2. Make a fumet, using the above ingredients (see p. 149).
3. Strain the fumet and pour into a large clean saucepan.
4. Simmer the potatoes in the fumet for 10 minutes.
5. Add the fish and continue to simmer for 5 to 10 minutes, until the fish is cooked.
6. Carefully remove the fish and the potatoes from the fumet and keep them warm on a serving dish.
7. In a clean saucepan, melt the butter and stir in the flour to make a roux.
8. Whisking all the time, gradually add the strained fish fumet to make a velouté sauce.
9. Allow the sauce to cook well, so that the taste of flour disappears completely.
10. Continue to add stock until the sauce becomes a creamy consistency.
11. Correct the seasoning.
12. Rub the bread with the garlic and sprinkle with salt. Dry it out in a slow oven, to make the croûtons.
13. Place the croûtons in a soup tureen, pour the creamy fish soup over, and serve.
14. This soup is followed by the fish and potatoes, moistened by a little stock.

Croûtes aux Champignons de Montargis
Mushroom rolls

Serves 6-8

250 g (8 oz) mushrooms, sliced
90 g (3 oz) butter
¼ cup (1 oz) flour

1 cup (8 fl oz) milk
salt and pepper
6-8 round bread rolls

1. Simmer the sliced mushrooms in 60 g of the butter for 5 minutes.
2. Melt the remaining butter in a saucepan, add the flour and make a roux.
3. Add the milk, salt and pepper, and stir briskly with a wire whisk until the sauce is thick.
4. Add the mushrooms and their liquid to the sauce and cook together gently for a few minutes.
5. Warm the rolls in the oven. When they are crisp, slice them open and remove the soft centre.
6. Butter the hollowed out rolls lightly and heat again.
7. Spoon the mushroom mixture into the hollowed out rolls and serve.

Chou Vert Farci
Braised and stuffed green cabbage

Serves 6-8

30 g (1 oz) butter
1 large onion, finely chopped
1 cup (2 oz) fresh white breadcrumbs
1 cup (8 fl oz) beef stock
500 g (1 lb) fresh minced pork
1 clove garlic, crushed
rosemary

thyme
4 tablespoons finely chopped parsley
salt and pepper
1 egg
1 cabbage
4 strips streaky (fat) bacon

1. Melt the butter, add the onion and cook slowly together until tender but not browned.
2. Soak the breadcrumbs in ½ cup of beef stock for 5 minutes. Drain through a sieve, pressing out as much liquid as possible.
3. Place the onions and the breadcrumbs in a mixing bowl.
4. Add the minced pork, garlic, rosemary, thyme, parsley, salt, pepper and egg and beat vigorously together.
5. Preheat the oven to 160°C (325°F).
6. Blanch a whole cabbage in salted water for several minutes.
7. Place it under the cold tap, drain it well and remove the stem.
8. Spread out the cabbage, starting with the outer leaves.
9. Remove the inner heart, chop it finely and add to the forcemeat stuffing.
10. Stuff the heart first with a ball of the forcemeat stuffing. Close the leaves around this.
11. Fill the next layer of leaves and close them, and so on, reforming the shape of the cabbage.
12. Wrap the cabbage in thin strips of bacon, and tie it with string to keep its shape.
13. Carefully transfer the stuffed cabbage to a heavy braising pan.
14. Pour the remaining ½ cup of stock over it, cover the pan and braise gently in the oven for 45 minutes.
15. Drain the cabbage and carefully transfer it to a round serving dish. Untie it.
16. Reduce the cooking liquid over a high heat, and pour a little over the cabbage. Serve the rest separately.

Rillettes de Tours

Potted pork rillettes
This recipe comes from Restaurant Le Calandre in Le Mans.

Serves 6-8

1 kg (2 lb) pork neck
90 g (3 oz) finest lard
¼ cup (2 fl oz) water

salt and pepper
1 teaspoon mixed spice

1. Cut up the fresh pork neck into small pieces.
2. Melt 30 g of the lard in a heavy pan with a lid.
3. Add the pork pieces and cook lightly, turning often.
4. Add the water, and cook gently with the lid on the pan, for 3 hours, stirring frequently to make sure the meat does not stick to the bottom of the pan. The mixture is ready when the meat flakes into pieces under the pressure of a fork.
5. Drain the pieces of pork and reserve any liquid.
6. Skim the fat off the liquid and add to the pork.
7. Season with salt, pepper and mixed spice, and pound the mixture finely.
8. Pour this mixture into small individual pots.
9. In a clean saucepan, melt the remaining 60 g of lard.
10. Cover each pot with a thin layer of lard, and chill well.

Friture de la Loire

Deep fried fingerlings
The River Loire and its many tributaries abound with fish. Crisp deep fried fingerlings is a well-known first course from this region.

Serves 6-8

1 cup (4 oz) flour
2 tablespoons olive oil
salt and pepper
8 tablespoons warm water
1 egg white

1 kg (2 lb) fingerlings (any small fish measuring approximately 2½-5 cm (1-2 in) long are suitable, such as whitebait, sardines etc.)
oil for deep frying

1. Blend together the flour, olive oil, salt, pepper and water to make a smooth batter.
2. Whip the egg white until it is stiff.
3. Fold the egg white into the batter mixture with a metal spoon.
4. Rinse and dry the small fish thoroughly; they need no cleaning.
5. Dust the fish with flour and dip them in the batter mixture.
6. Deep fry the fish in the preheated oil for two or three minutes, until they are cooked. (It is a good idea to deep fry the fingerlings a cup at a time, so they do not stick together.)
6. Drain them well, arrange on a warm plate and garnish with lemon wedges.
7. Serve immediately.

La Calandre, Le Mans.
The province of Maine, like that of Anjou, is famous for its charcuterie. At Le Mans, chef Madelenat's specialities are rillettes and rillons. (Rillons are fresh breasts of pork cut into small pieces, seasoned with rock salt and left to pickle for 12 hours. They are then cooked in lard. They are very rich but delicious.) He is also famous for 'Tarte aux Rillettes', his own creation.

Above: *A selection of dishes from La Calandre in Le Mans. Clockwise from bottom left: boiled vegetables, sausages, tart of rillettes, rillettes and rillons.*

Farci de Poitou
Stuffed braised lettuce leaves

Serves 6-8

1 kg (2 lb) minced pork belly
2 eggs, beaten
1 small bunch sorrel, chopped
2 cloves garlic, crushed
salt and freshly ground black pepper

pinch of allspice
pinch of cayenne pepper
1 lettuce, with the leaves separated
3 cups (24 fl oz) chicken stock

1. In a mixing bowl, combine the minced pork, eggs, sorrel, garlic, salt, pepper and spices.
2. Blanch the lettuce leaves in boiling water and drain.
3. Finely chop the small lettuce heart leaves and add to the meat mixture.
4. Place a tablespoon of the meat mixture on each lettuce leaf and roll up tightly. Squeeze the rolls in your hand to ensure the stuffing stays enclosed.
5. In a large saucepan, heat the chicken stock to boiling point.
6. Gently lower the lettuce rolls into the stock and simmer until cooked through – approximately 20 minutes.
7. Drain well. This dish may be served either hot or cold.

Oeufs Belle Angevine
Hard boiled eggs baked Angevine style

Serves 6

12 eggs
2 cups (16 fl oz) Béchamel sauce
  (see p. 147)
1 tablespoon parsley, chopped

1 tablespoon chives, chopped
125 g (4 oz) butter, softened
2 tablespoons cream

1. Preheat the oven to 190°C (375°F).
2. Hard boil the eggs (at least 12 minutes).
3. Prepare the Béchamel sauce.
4. Cool the eggs, remove from the shell, cut them in half and take out the yolks.
5. Blend the yolks with the parsley, chives, softened butter and 3 tablespoons of the cooled Béchamel sauce.
6. Fill the egg whites with this mixture.
7. Add any egg mixture left over to the Béchamel, together with the cream and heat through, but do not boil.
8. Place the stuffed eggs on an ovenproof dish and cover with the enriched sauce.
9. Bake for 15 minutes.
10. Serve in the dish in which it was cooked.

Mouclade Maraichine

Mussels in cream sauce
The Marais Poitevin is a huge coastal hinterland of fertile flatlands and marshes, drained by many little canals and rivers. Excellent shellfish and mussels are found in this region, and this is a delicious yet simple recipe found locally.

Serves 6

1.5 kg (3 lb) mussels (allow 250 g (8 oz) per person)
3 onions, chopped
3 tablespoons finely chopped parsley
3 teaspoons curry powder

salt and freshly ground black pepper
3 cups (24 fl oz) white wine
3 cups (24 fl oz) cream
chopped fresh parsley to garnish

1. Scrub and thoroughly wash the mussels.
2. Place all the ingredients, except the parsley for the garnish, in a large covered saucepan and cook over a brisk heat, shaking the pan often until all the mussels are open. This will take 5-6 minutes.
3. With a perforated spoon, remove the mussels from the pan.
4. Let the sauce simmer gently until it is reduced to a thick creamy consistency.
5. Remove the empty half shells, and arrange the mussels in their half shells on a warmed serving dish.
6. Correct the seasoning of the sauce.
7. Pour the hot sauce over the mussels and sprinkle with chopped parsley. Serve immediately as a first course.

Brème Farcie

Stuffed Bream
Local gourmets maintain that the River Indre, one of the tributaries of the Loire, provides the best carp and bream in the district. Stuffed bream is a popular way of serving this fish.

Serves 6-8

1 bream per person
2 medium-sized onions, finely chopped
2 tablespoons oil
250 g (8 oz) mushrooms, chopped
1 garlic clove, crushed
3 tablespoons fine fresh breadcrumbs
1 tablespoon chopped chives

1 tablespoon chopped parsley
milk
salt and pepper
bouquet garni
1½ cups (12 fl oz) dry white wine
30 g (1 oz) butter

1. Preheat the oven to 190°C (375°F).
2. Clean and scale the bream.
3. Fry the onions in the oil until they are transparent.
4. Add the mushrooms and garlic, and cook for five minutes, stirring often.
5. Remove the pan from the heat. Add the breadcrumbs, chives and parsley.
6. Moisten and bind the stuffing mixture with a little milk.
7. Add salt and pepper to taste.
8. Stuff each fish with the mixture.
9. Place the fish in an ovenproof dish. Add the bouquet garni and wine, and dot with butter.
10. Cook in the oven until tender, basting frequently with the juice. this will take about 15 minutes.
11. Drain the fish and place on a warm serving dish.
12. Reduce the liquid over a hot stove to make a light sauce, or serve with a Beurre Blanc sauce (see page 96).

Terrine de Canard a l'Orange

Terrine of duckling with orange
This recipe comes from the Hôtel Terminus in Niort.

Serves 12

1 kg (2 lb) duck meat, boned
  and chopped
1 kg (2 lb) minced pork
4 eggs

finely grated rind of 2 oranges
salt and freshly ground black pepper
pinch of allspice
½ cup (4 fl oz) rum

1. Preheat the oven to 180°C (350°F).
2. Blend the duck meat, pork, eggs, orange rind, salt, pepper, allspice and rum until they are all well mixed.
3. Transfer to a well buttered terrine dish and cover.
4. Stand the terrine in a dish of simmering water, and cook in the oven for 1½ hours.
5. Allow to cool, and chill well before serving.

Brochet à la Marinière

Pike with marinière sauce
If pike is unobtainable, substitute snapper, whiting or any other white-fleshed fish.

Serves 6-8

1 pike, approximately 2 kg (4 lb)
2 onions, sliced
2 spring onions (scallions), quartered
2 cloves garlic
chives
4 sprigs of parsley
1 sprig of thyme
1 small bay leaf
salt and pepper
white wine to cover

Sauce:
1 tablespoon chopped spring onions
  (scallions)
125 g (4 oz) butter
½ cup (4 fl oz) dry white wine
1½ cups (12 fl oz) fish fumet
  (see p. 149)
¼ cup (1 oz) flour
2 egg yolks, beaten
1 tablespoon finely chopped parsley
mussels (optional)

1. Place the cleaned, well washed fish into a fish kettle, surrounded with the onions, spring onions, garlic, chives, parsley, thyme, bay leaf, salt and pepper.
2. Cover with wine and leave to marinate for one hour.
3. About ¾ hour before serving, put the fish kettle on the heat. As soon as the liquid begins to boil, turn the heat down and simmer until the fish is cooked.

Sauce:
1. Meanwhile in a saucepan, cook the spring onions in 1 tablespoon of the butter without letting it colour.
2. Add the wine, and ½ cup of fish fumet, and boil down until it is reduced by half.
3. In a clean saucepan, melt another tablespoon of butter. Add the flour to make a roux.
4. Add the remaining fish fumet, stirring well with a wire whisk, and add this sauce to the reduced wine and fumet mixture.
5. Remove from the heat, and whisk in the egg yolks.
6. Return the pan to a low heat and gradually add the remaining butter, stirring constantly.
7. Add the parsley.

To serve:
1. When the fish is cooked, gently remove it from the fish kettle, drain it well and place it on a warmed serving dish.
2. Cover the fish with the sauce, to which may be added a few cooked mussels if desired, and serve.

Hôtel Terminus, Niort.
Poitou is not one of the better known gastronomic areas of France and its cuisine is characterised by its simplicity. The Terminus serves wholesome, bourgeois food which makes the most of the good quality local produce, especially poultry and pork.

Above: *Duck Terrine, as prepared at the Hôtel Terminus in Niort.*

Champignons avec Beurre d'Escargot

Baked mushrooms with snail butter
The mushrooms of the Touraine are big field mushrooms. They are served inverted on slices of toasted French bread, brimming with snail butter, and form an accompaniment to the roasts for which this region is famous.

Serves 6-8

12-16 large mushroom caps
185 g (6 oz) butter, softened
2 tablespoons finely chopped spring
  onions (scallions)

1 large clove garlic, crushed
1 tablespoon chopped parsley
salt and pepper
12-16 slices of French bread, toasted

1. Preheat the oven to 200°C (400°F).
2. Wash and dry the mushrooms.
3. Place the butter, spring onions, garlic and parsley in a bowl. Season with salt and freshly ground black pepper and blend well.
4. Lightly toast the rounds of French bread.
5. Arrange the toasted rounds of French bread on a baking tray. Place one mushroom hollow side up on each round of bread.
6. Place a generous teaspoon of the butter mixture in each mushroom cap.
7. Cook the mushrooms in the oven for 5 to 7 minutes, or until the butter is melted, and the mushrooms are just cooked.
8. Serve immediately.

Matelote d'Anguilles

Fish stew with onions and mushrooms
Traditionally, Matelote d'Anguilles is prepared with fresh eel poached in red wine, but this recipe may be adapted to any firm-fleshed fish, such as gemfish, haddock, jewfish or monkfish.

Serves 6-8

2-3 kg (4-6 lb) fish, scaled, cleaned and
  heads and tails removed
2 tablespoons oil
125 g (4 oz) butter
250 g (8 oz) small onions, peeled and
  left whole

250 g (8 oz) mushrooms
bouquet garni
salt and pepper
red wine
1 tablespoon flour

1. Cut the fish into pieces of equal thickness, and fry in the oil and half the butter in a heavy pan.
2. Add the onions, mushrooms, bouquet garni, salt and pepper and moisten with red wine. (The fish should not be quite covered.)
3. Simmer very gently for 15 minutes, or until the fish is cooked.
4. Remove the bouquet garni.
5. Drain the pieces of fish, the mushrooms and the onions, and keep them warm on a serving dish while preparing the sauce.
6. Reduce the fish stock by boiling vigorously until it is two thirds the original volume.
7. In a clean saucepan, melt the remaining butter, stir in the flour, and add the strained fish stock to make a slightly thickened sauce.
8. Pour the sauce over the fish pieces, the onions and the mushrooms, and serve immediately.

Rognons de Veau Sauté Vallée de Cousse

Veal kidneys in red wine and mustard sauce

Serves 6-8

6-8 veal kidneys
100 g (3½ oz) butter
125 g (4 oz) bacon, finely diced
2 onions, finely chopped
250 g (8 oz) button mushrooms
salt and pepper

1 clove garlic, crushed
pinch of dried tarragon
1¼ cups (10 fl oz) red wine
1 tablespoon French mustard
2 tablespoons cream
finely chopped fresh parsley

1. Trim all the fat and sinew from the kidneys, and slice them.
2. Melt the butter in a heavy pan, and fry the kidneys over a brisk heat for 3 to 4 minutes, turning them once.
3. Remove the kidneys with a slotted spoon from the pan to a serving dish and keep them warm.
4. Sauté the bacon, onions and mushrooms in the same pan until lightly browned.
5. Add the salt, pepper, garlic and tarragon, and cook gently.
6. Stir in the red wine, and simmer to reduce the sauce slightly.
7. Add the mustard, and then the cream. Blend the sauce well, but do not allow it to boil.
8. When the sauce is heated through, pour it over the kidneys, sprinkle with chopped parsley and serve immediately.

Noix de Veau Braisée

Rump of veal braised in white wine
The noix of veal is the topside, the fleshy upper part of the leg, cut lengthwise.

Serves 6-8

125 g (4 oz) larding bacon, cut into
   thin strips
several sprigs of fresh (if possible)
   rosemary
½ cup (4 fl oz) dry white wine
1 nut of veal, about 2 kg (3½ to 4 lb)

60 g (2 oz) butter
2 onions, thinly sliced
2 carrots, thinly sliced
½ cup (4 fl oz) chicken stock
bouquet garni
salt and freshly ground black pepper

1. Marinate the strips of bacon and the sprigs of rosemary for several hours in the wine.
2. Preheat the oven to 160°C (325°F).
3. Drain the bacon and rosemary and reserve the wine.
4. Trim the meat and stud the joint with the strips of bacon and sprigs of rosemary.
5. Melt the butter in a heavy casserole dish, and brown the veal on all sides. Remove from the dish.
6. In the same melted butter, gently fry the sliced onions and carrots, and also any bacon rind which may have been cut off the bacon.
7. When the vegetables have softened, return the veal to the dish and add the stock and the wine.
8. Add the bay leaf and season with salt and freshly ground black pepper.
9. Bring the liquid to the boil.
10. Cover the dish and cook the veal in the preheated oven for 1¼ hours, basting frequently.
11. Half an hour before the end of the cooking time, remove the cover so that the meat browns a little.
12. When the veal is cooked, remove the joint from the casserole dish and keep it warm.
13. Reduce the liquid in the dish over a high flame, and correct the seasoning. Strain and serve with the meat.

Pâté de Veau et Lapereau à la Solognote

Veal and rabbit pie
The Orléanais was originally the main source of game in France, supplying it to many of the great aristocratic houses. Today some of the towns of this region are still well known for game pâtés and terrines.

Serves 12

Pastry:
750 g (1½ lb) flour
2 teaspoons salt
90 g (3 oz) butter
90 g (3 oz) lard
1 scant cup (8 fl oz) hot water
1 teaspoon oil

Filling:
1 large rabbit
375 g (12 oz) sausage meat
1 tablespoon chopped parsley
1 cup (2 oz) fresh breadcrumbs
pinch of dried thyme
salt and pepper
375 g (12 oz) lean veal
slices of streaky (fat) bacon
2 sprigs fresh thyme
1 egg yolk, beaten.

Pastry:
1. Put the flour in a bowl and mix in the salt.
2. Melt the butter and the lard in the hot water, and then add the oil.
3. Make a well in the middle of the flour and pour in the water and fat mixture.
4. Mix the dough well and knead it.
5. Smear the inside of a 23 cm (9 in) cake tin with butter and line with long strips of foil, so the pâté may be lifted out. (Since a heavy pie cooked in a tin can be difficult to get out, a spring-form cake tin is ideal for such pâtés as this one).
6. Divide the dough into two, and divide one part in half again.
7. Roll out one of these small pieces to form the base of the pie, and press into place.
8. Roll the large piece into a rectangle the height of the tin to form the sides. Dampen the joins and press firmly together. Chill while preparing the filling.

Filling:
1. Bone the rabbit and cut out any sinews. Cut the meat into small pieces.
2. Mix the sausage meat with the chopped parsley and breadcrumbs in a bowl. Season well and add some thyme.
3. Cut the veal into small chunks.

Assembly:
1. Preheat the oven to 180°C (350°F).
2. Line the inside of the pie with a few slices of bacon.
3. Sprinkle in some of the sausage meat mixture.
4. Lay on some rabbit pieces, then some veal chunks, and then some more sausage meat mixture.
5. Continue these layers until the pie is full. Finish with sausage meat and two slices of bacon.
6. Lay on the sprigs of thyme and cover the pie with the remaining small piece of pastry, sealing the joins well.
7. Brush the pie with beaten egg yolk, and decorate if desired with off-cuts of pastry.
8. Cut a small hole in the top and bake the pie for 1½ hours.
9. After half the cooking time, cover the pie with a piece of foil. When some clear liquid starts to come out of the hole, the pie is cooked. (Test for tenderness with a skewer to be sure).
10. Let the pie cool, before removing it from the tin.
11. Serve cold, in slices.

La Fricassée Poitevine

Chicken fricassée Poitou style
There are extensive poultry farms in the fertile Poitou district, and Fricassée Poitevine is
frequently found on local menus.

Serves 4

185 g (6 oz) unsalted butter
1 large chicken, jointed
1 kg (2 lb) onions, finely chopped

1 kg (2 lb) tomatoes, peeled, seeded
  and chopped
3 cloves garlic, chopped
salt and freshly ground black pepper

1. Preheat the oven to 180°C (350°F).
2. Heat half the butter in a heavy frying pan and fry the chicken pieces over medium heat for 15 minutes, turning them so that they become brown on both sides.
3. At the same time, in another frying pan, heat the rest of the butter and fry the onions until they are transparent, but not brown.
4. Add the tomatoes and garlic to the onions and cook over a low heat for 10 minutes.
5. Season well with salt and pepper.
6. Butter an earthenware casserole generously.
7. Cover the bottom of the casserole with the onions and tomatoes, and arrange the chicken pieces on top.
8. Cover the casserole and braise the chicken in the oven for about 25 minutes, or until the chicken is tender.
9. Adjust the seasoning and serve the chicken in the casserole.

Noisettes de Porc aux Pruneaux

Loin fillets of pork with prunes and cream sauce

Serves 6-8

approximately 3 dozen large dried
  prunes, pitted
1½ cups (12 fl oz) dry white wine
4-6 pork fillets, trimmed and sliced
  3.5 cm (1½ in) thick
salt and pepper
flour

80 g (2½ oz) butter
2 tablespoons oil
1 cup (8 fl oz) chicken stock
1¼ cups (10 fl oz) cream
1 tablespoon redcurrant jelly
1 teaspoon lemon juice

1. Marinate the prunes in the white wine at room temperature for several hours, or overnight if possible.
2. Cook the prunes and the wine over a moderate heat for 10 minutes.
3. Drain, and put the prunes and wine aside separately.
4. Season the noisettes of pork with salt and pepper, and dust with flour.
5. Melt the butter with the oil in a heavy pan, and sauté the noisettes for about 3 minutes on each side until they are browned. Transfer them from the pan to a plate.
6. Pour off almost all the fat from the pan. Add the wine in which the prunes have been cooked, and boil it briskly until it has reduced to 1 tablespoon.
7. Pour in the chicken stock and bring the liquid to the boil again.
8. Return the noisettes to the pan, cover, and simmer very gently over a low heat for about 15-20 minutes, or until the noisettes are tender.
9. Transfer the noisettes from the pan to a serving dish, and keep warm.
10. Thoroughly degrease the stock remaining in the pan. Pour in the cream and bring it to the boil, stirring and scraping in any brown bits.
11. Boil the sauce briskly, stirring constantly, until it is thick enough to coat the back of a spoon.
12. Stir in the prunes, redcurrant jelly and lemon juice and cook until the jelly is dissolved and the prunes heated through.
13. Taste and correct the seasoning.
14. Arrange the prunes around the noisettes, spoon the sauce over the top and serve at once.

Gâteau de Pithiviers

Pithiviers almond cake
Pithiviers is famous for its almond flavoured pastry and cakes, and this recipe is typical of this region.

Makes 1 20 cm (8 in) cake

2 eggs, separated
¾ cup (6 oz) sugar
1 teaspoon vanilla essence
90 g (3 oz) butter, softened
1⅔ cup (6 oz) ground almonds

Icing:
¾ cup (4 oz) icing (confectioners)
 sugar
1 egg white
glazed fruit peel

1. Preheat the oven to 160°C (325°F).
2. Beat the egg yolks, sugar and vanilla essence together.
3. In another bowl, mix the butter with the ground almonds.
4. Combine all these ingredients together.
5. Whip the egg whites until stiff, and fold into the cake mixture.
6. Grease a 20 cm (8 in) cake tin and fill with the mixture.
7. Bake for 20 minutes.

Icing:
1. When the cake is cool, make an icing by stirring the icing sugar into a lightly beaten egg white, to make a spreading mixture.
2. Spread the top of the cake with the icing mixture.
3. Sprinkle the cake with glazed fruit peel.

Tourteau Fromage

Typical of this region is this baked cheesecake, made in Poitou from goat's cheese, but where this is unobtainable, fresh cream cheese may be substituted.

Makes 1 x 22 cm (9 in) tart

250 g (8 oz) short crust pastry
 (see p. 150)
185 g (6 oz) fresh cream cheese
3 eggs

½ cup (4 oz) sugar
2 tablespoons cream
2 tablespoons chopped angelica

1. Preheat oven to 150°C (300°F).
2. Prepare the short crust pastry.
3. Mix together the cream cheese, eggs, sugar, cream and angelica until the ingredients are well blended.
4. Line the tart dish with the rolled out pastry.
5. Fill with the cheese mixture.
6. Bake the tart for about 40 minutes.
7. Allow the tart to cool before serving.

Citrouillat

Pumpkin pie

Serves 6-8

500 g (1 lb) pumpkin, chopped
60 g (2 oz) butter
20 prunes, soaked and stoned
½ cup (4 fl oz) cream

¼ cup (2 oz) sugar
250 g (8 oz) short crust pastry
(see p. 150)

1. Preheat the oven to 190°C (375°F).
2. Cook the chopped pumpkin in the butter until reduced to a purée. Blend well.
3. Add the drained and stoned prunes, the cream and sugar and mix well.
4. Make the short crust pastry.
5. Roll it out and cut it into two rounds the size of the pie dish.
6. Line the greased dish with one round, and fill with the pumpkin mixture.
7. Cover with the second round of pastry, dampening the edges and pressing firmly together.
8. Make a small hole in the top, and bake for 10 minutes, then reduce the heat to 160°C (325°F) for a further 20 minutes.
9. Serve hot with cream.

Macarons

Macaroons
The Touraine is renowned for its cookies and barley sugars, but the particular speciality of the small town of Ligueil is macaroons.

Approximately 3 dozen small macaroons

250 g (8 oz) ground almonds
250 g (8 oz) sugar

2 egg whites, beaten
1 teaspoon vanilla essence
oil

1. Preheat the oven to 180°C (350°F).
2. Mix the ground almonds with the sugar.
3. Beat the egg whites until they are stiff.
4. Stir the egg whites into the sugar and almond mixture and flavour with the vanilla essence.
5. Line a baking sheet with greaseproof paper and oil lightly.
6. Make small balls of the mixture with oiled teaspoons and drop on to the baking tray.
7. Bake for 20 minutes. When removed from the oven, the macaroons will appear to be soft, but they will harden when cooled.
8. Turn over the paper with the macaroons attached, and peel off gently. If it sticks, moisten the paper with a clean sponge until the macaroons slip off.

Île-de-France

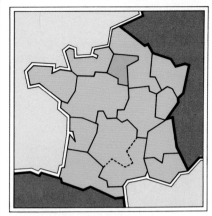

It is rather difficult to try to analyse and assess the regional food of the Île-de-France. Many of the dishes now regarded as Île-de-France specialities were brought to Paris in the 16th Century by the Italian chefs and pastry-cooks who accompanied Catherine and Maria dei Medici. Others originated in the provinces and now, under different names, appear as specialities of the capital.

But Paris has had its share of culinary innovations too: the court chef under Charles VI was responsible for the creation of entremets (between meats), sweet dishes served between the many courses, then so fashionable. Deep-frying is a speciality of the region and the vol-au-vent originated here.

Many dishes have been created by the numerous and famous restaurants of the capital: Sole Marguéry, Potage Germiny, an egg-yolk-cream sorrel soup first cooked by Duglère at the Café Anglais, Pressed Duck Tour d'Argent, to name the best known.

There are dishes which bear the names of places in the region such as Potage Saint-Germain, Matelote de Beavais and the various poultry pâtés, those of Laon, Hondon and Étamps.

Today, many of the preparations bearing the name 'à la Parisienne' are served with various vegetables, including small cubed potatoes (parmentier), sautéed in butter, glazed with veal stock and sprinkled with parsley. (It was through Antoine Parmentier's endeavours in the 18th Century that potatoes were made popular as a food.) Sauce Béarnaise is the creation of the Pavillion Henry IV Restaurant located not far from Paris and honours the country where Henry IV was born. The Châteaubriand is considered an Île-de-France speciality.

Many charcuterie preparations are of Parisian origin: Hure de porc Parisienne, Pâté de Porc de Paris and the elegant Jambon Glacé de Paris.

The regions around Paris grow very good vegetables: champignons de Paris, asparagus of Argenteuil, peas of Clamart, string beans from Bagnolet and the famous Crécy carrots. One of the most famous products of the province is the cheese of Brie.

Whatever its origins, the food of Paris at its best is unsurpassed. It perpetuates the long-established traditions first created at the table of kings, then continued in the 18th Century on a modest scale in the newly established restaurants, and today a simplified and refined version is available in many of the world's best eating places.

Sweet stall on the streets of Paris.

Potage Parmentier

Thick potato soup
Hearty nourishing soups using potatoes are very popular in this region, particularly during the colder weather.

Serves 6-8

2 leeks
90 g (3 oz) butter
500 g (1 lb) potatoes, cut in quarters
4 cups (1 litre) chicken stock

salt and pepper
4 tablespoons cream
1 tablespoon fresh chervil leaves

1. Shred the white part of the leeks and cook them lightly in 30 g of the butter.
2. Add the potatoes.
3. Pour in the chicken stock, bring it to the boil, and simmer until the potatoes are cooked (about 15 minutes). Add salt and pepper to taste.
4. As soon as the potatoes are cooked, mash them thoroughly, and put the soup through a sieve.
5. Stir in the cream, the remaining butter and the chervil leaves and heat through.

Note: Potage Parmentier may be served with small croûtons, fried in butter.

Potage Saint Germain

St Germain soup
This is one of the best known French soups, a thick fresh pea soup, which may be garnished with chopped ham.

Serves 6-8

750 g (1½ lb) shelled or frozen peas
4-5 cups (1-1.25 litres) chicken stock
salt and pepper

1 teaspoon dried chervil
60 g (2 oz) butter
1 tablespoon chopped ham

1. Cook the peas in salted water, and drain well.
2. Reserve 2 tablespoons of the peas for the garnish.
3. Purée the remaining peas, either in an electric blender, or with a sieve.
4. Dilute the purée with the chicken stock and bring it to the boil.
5. Season with the salt, pepper and chervil.
6. Finish the soup off by stirring in the butter, and garnish with the reserved peas and the chopped ham.

Petits Pois à la Française

French style fresh garden peas

Serves 4

500 g (1 lb) shelled or frozen peas
1 lettuce heart, shredded
12 small onions, peeled
bouquet garni

90 g (3 oz) + 3 teaspoons butter
1 teaspoon salt
2 teaspoons sugar
3 tablespoons cold water

1. Choose a deep saucepan, and place in it the peas, lettuce heart, onions, bouquet garni, 90 g of the butter, salt and sugar and stir to mix all the ingredients.
2. Add the water and bring to the boil.
3. Simmer gently with the lid on until the peas are cooked, (about 15 minutes).
4. At the last moment, when the peas are cooked, remove the bouquet garni, take the saucepan off the heat, stir in the remaining 3 teaspoon of butter, and serve.

Pâté de Porc
Pork Pâté

Makes about 1.5 kg (3 lb)

1 kg (2 lb) fresh pork neck
500 g (1 lb) pigs' liver
1 large onion, finely chopped
1 clove garlic, crushed
1 bayleaf
1 tablespoon fresh sage, finely
  chopped (or ½ teaspoon dried sage)

pinch of allspice
salt and pepper
1 tablespoon brandy
125 g (4 oz) bacon strips, or thin strips
  of pork fat
3 tablespoons dry white wine

1. Finely mince the meat and the liver.
2. Add the onion, garlic, bayleaf, sage, spice, salt and pepper.
3. Pour the brandy over the mixture, stir well and marinate in a cool place for 24 hours.
4. Preheat the oven to 180°C (350°F).
5. Line the bottom and sides of the terrine with the bacon, or pork fat.
6. Add the white wine to the meat mixture.
7. Spoon the meat mixture into the terrine and cover with a further layer of bacon or pork fat.
8. Enclose the top of the terrine with foil, cover and place in a pan of boiling water (the water should come half way up the side of the terrine).
9. Place in the lower part of the oven, and bake for about 1½ hours. (The pâté is done when it has shrunk slightly from the sides of the terrine, and the surrounding fat and juices run clear. It may be necessary to top up the boiling water during cooking.)
10. Take the terrine from the water and place it on a plate.
11. Remove the lid and place a weight which just fits into the terrine on top of the foil. This will compress the pâté so there will be no air spaces in the meat.
12. Allow the pâté to cool, then chill it, still weighted down, and keep for a couple of days in the refrigerator before serving.
13. The pâté may be served either from the terrine, sliced downwards, or unmoulded on a dish, and decorated as desired.

Friands Parisiens
Savoury meat rolls

Makes approximately 2 dozen friands

500 g (1 lb) best available pork
  sausage meat
2 tablespoons finely chopped parsley
1 tablespoon finely chopped sage

salt and pepper
1 teaspoon lemon juice
250 g (8 oz) puff pastry (see page 150)
1 egg beaten

1. Preheat the oven to 190°C (375°F).
2. Mash the sausage meat with the chopped parsley, sage, salt, pepper and lemon juice until all the ingredients are well blended.
3. Roll out the puff pastry and cut it into strips about 7.5 cm (3 in) wide.
4. Place a spoonful of the stuffing on the end of one strip of pastry, roll it over once and cut across the pastry.
5. Dampen the edges with water before pressing together.
6. Brush with beaten egg and place on a baking tray.
7. Continue in the same way, until you have used all the meat.
8. Bake the savoury rolls for 20 minutes.

Canard Braisé à l'Orange

Braised duck with orange sauce
This recipe comes from the Restaurant Lasserre in Paris.

Serves 3

60 g (2 oz) butter
2 kg (4 lb) duck
⅓ cup (2½ fl oz) Cointreau liqueur
½ tablespoon sugar
½ tablespoon white wine vinegar
⅔ cup (5 fl oz) orange juice

⅔ cup (5 fl oz) brown stock
salt
freshly ground pepper
¼ cup (2 fl oz) mandarine liqueur
6 large ripe oranges

1. Preheat the oven to 180°C (375°F).
2. In a heavy bottomed casserole, melt the butter and brown the duck. Cover the pan and braise the duck for 45 minutes in the oven.
3. Add the Cointreau and continue braising for a further few minutes.
4. Remove the duck to another covered dish and keep hot.
5. Return the casserole to the top of the stove, add the sugar, vinegar, orange juice and the brown stock and gently cook for about 10 minutes.
6. Degrease and pass through a fine cheesecloth. Season, add the mandarine liqueur and set aside.
7. Peel the oranges and divide each into 8 segments.
8. Place the segments in a saucepan and pour over the reserved sauce.
9. Gently heat them for about 2 minutes over a very low flame.
10. Serve the duck on a decorative platter with some of the sauce poured over it and half of the orange segments arranged around it. Serve the remainder of the sauce with the rest of the orange segments in a sauce boat.

Casserole de Filets de Sole 'Lasserre'

Pastry cases filled with poached fillets of sole 'Lasserre'
A speciality of the Restaurant Lasserre in Paris.

Serves 4

2 soles, filleted (if sole is
** unobtainable, substitute John Dory)**
fumet (made from the sole trimmings,
** ½ cup (4 fl oz) white wine, 3 finely**
** chopped mushrooms and 1 spring**
** onion, (scallion) chopped,**
** (see page 149)**
1 tablespoon cream

70 g (2½ oz) butter
2 egg yolks
4 individual baked pastry shells
8 button mushrooms, finely chopped
** and cooked in a little butter**
5 asparagus tips, cooked
salt and freshly ground black pepper

1. Preheat the oven to 230°C (450°F).
2. Cut each sole fillet into three equal parts.
3. Make the fish fumet.
4. Arrange the fillets in an ovenproof dish.
5. Pour the fumet over the fish and cook in the oven uncovered, for 7 to 10 minutes.
6. Drain the fillets well and keep them warm.
7. Add the cream to the cooking liquid, and reduce by three quarters.
8. Remove from the heat and beat in the butter.
9. Beat in the egg yolks and cook, whisking continuously in a double saucepan.
10. Place a spoonful of the cooked, finely chopped mushrooms in the bottom of each of the pastry cases.
11. Add the asparagus tips.
12. Arrange the sole fillets on the top.
13. Cover with the sauce, and glaze under a hot grill until golden. Serve very hot.
14. Lasserre fixes a small pastry 'handle' to each tart to form a casserolette.

Restaurant Lasserre, Paris.
The three stars and five red forks of the Michelin Guide are the highest recommendation a restaurant can receive. Founded by its owner René Lasserre in 1945, its reputation as one of the premier restaurants of France is based on infinite care and constancy in the preparation of food in the best of French culinary tradition, a reputation which so far has not been surpassed. Lasserre not only presents perfect examples from the classical, traditional repertoire but has developed its own specialities, such as the Pigeon 'André Malraux' and 'Casserol de Filets de Sole Lasserre'.

Above: *Clockwise from bottom left: Fillets of Sole in pastry cases, Duck with Orange, Fish Croquettes, Stuffed Pigeons (p. 120).*

Filets de Sole Grandgousier

Fillets of sole in tomato, champagne and mushroom sauce
If sole is unobtainable, substitute John Dory. This recipe comes from the Restaurant Chez Pauline in Paris.

Serves 4

2 sole, filleted
2 cups (16 fl oz) dry white wine
2 tablespoons Champagne
200 g (6½ oz) mushrooms,
  finely sliced
1 tablespoon tomato paste
250 g (8 oz) fresh tomatoes, peeled,
  seeded and chopped
125 g (4 oz) butter
salt and freshly ground black pepper
pinch of paprika

Garnish:
2 artichoke hearts, cut in quarters
8 prawns, peeled
fleurons (small puff pastry shapes)

1. Pound the fish fillets gently to flatten them slightly and rinse them in cold water.
2. Dry them well, and fold in two.
3. Place the fish fillets, white wine, champagne and mushrooms in a pan and poach the fish very gently.
4. Remove the fillets and keep warm.
5. Reduce the cooking fluid by three quarters over a high flame.
6. Add the tomato paste and the fresh tomatoes.
7. Cook, stirring well until the sauce is a creamy texture.
8. Removing from the heat, beat in the butter.
9. Season with salt, freshly ground black pepper and paprika.
10. Arrange the fillets on a serving platter, and pour the sauce over the top.
11. Garnish with quarters of artichoke hearts which have been warmed in butter, decorated with the prawns, and the fleurons.
12. Serve immediately.

Tournedos Flambés Medicis

Tournedos with Béarnaise and Madeira Sauce

Serves 6-8

Sauce Béarnaise (see page 147)
1 tablespoon butter
6-8 tournedos
salt and pepper

3 tablespoons brandy, warmed
1 tablespoon Madeira
1 cup (8 fl oz) beef stock
sauce Madère (see page 149)

1. Prepare the Béarnaise sauce and reserve.
2. Heat a heavy bottomed pan and melt the butter.
3. Season the tournedos with freshly ground black pepper and fry in the hot butter until well browned (2 to 3 minutes on each side for rare tournedos).
4. Add the brandy to the pan and ignite, shaking the pan until the flames die out.
5. Remove the tournedos from the pan and keep them warm.
6. Dilute the pan juices with the Madeira and beef stock and proceed with the sauce Madère .

TO SERVE TOURNEDOS FLAMBÉS MEDICIS: The tournedos are served with a tablespoon of the Béarnaise sauce on the top, and with a little of the Madeira sauce poured around the meat.

Sole Maguery

Sole with mussels and prawns
This is named after the restaurant in Paris where this dish originated.

Serves 6-8

Allow 1 sole (or flounder) per person
1¼ cups (10 fl oz) fish fumet
  (see p. 149)
1 kg (2 lb) mussels
1 cup (8 fl oz) dry white wine

salt and pepper
250 g (8 oz) small prawns (shrimps)
6 egg yolks
375 g (12 oz) butter, softened

  1. Fillet the sole.
  2. Use the trimmings from the sole to make a fumet.
  3. Cook the mussels in the wine, salt and pepper until the shells open. Drain and strain the liquid.
  4. Combine the sole fumet and the mussel liquid.
  5. Place the fillets of sole, seasoned and lightly flattened, on a buttered baking dish.
  6. Sprinkle over a few tablespoons of fish fumet and poach gently for 5 minutes, covered with foil.
  7. Drain the fillets well, and arrange in an oval dish, surrounded by a double row of the shelled mussels and prawns. Cover and keep hot while preparing the sauce.
  8. Add the cooking juices to the fumet.
  9. Boil vigorously until the liquid is reduced by two thirds. Remove from the heat and allow to cool slightly.
  10. In a double saucepan, combine the egg yolks and the reduced fumet, whisking over hot, but not boiling, water.
  11. Gradually incorporate the butter, whisking all the time as if for a Hollandaise sauce, until the sauce thickens. (Never allow the water in the bottom saucepan to boil, or the sauce will curdle.)
  12. Correct the seasoning and pour the sauce over the sole fillets.
  13. Glaze in a hot oven for five minutes and serve.

La Fricassée de Poulet

Chicken with mushrooms and cream

Serves 4

125 g (4 oz) butter
1 large chicken, jointed
12 small white onions, peeled
250 g (8 oz) button mushrooms
2 cups (16 fl oz) dry white wine

1 cup (8 fl oz) chicken stock
2 cups (16 fl oz) cream
salt and freshly ground black pepper
finely chopped parsley

  1. Heat the butter in a heavy casserole dish and add the chicken pieces and the onions.
  2. Cook over a medium heat for 5 minutes without letting the chicken pieces take on any colour.
  3. Add the whole mushrooms, wine and stock, and simmer gently until the chicken is cooked (about 25 minutes).
  4. Transfer the chicken, onions and mushrooms to a serving dish and keep them warm.
  5. Pour the cream into the casserole dish and boil briskly for a few minutes.
  6. Adjust the seasoning and pour over the chicken.
  7. Serve, garnished with a little chopped parsley.

Jambon Persillé de Bourgogne

Ham in parsley jelly
From the Restaurant Chez Pauline in Paris.

Serves 6-8

1 ham, or piece of ham	5-6 spring onions (scallions), chopped
1 veal knuckle	2 bottles of white wine
2 calves' feet	6 tablespoons parsley, finely chopped
bouquet garni	1 teaspoon vinegar
fresh chervil	¼ cup (2 fl oz) white wine
fresh tarragon	salt and fresh ground black pepper

1. Soak the ham overnight. Drain.
2. Cover with fresh, cold water, bring to the boil.
3. Cook for 1 hour. Drain the ham and rinse in clean water.
4. Return the ham to the pan, and add the veal knuckle, calves' feet, bouquet garni, chervil, tarragon, spring onions and the two bottles of white wine.
5. Simmer gently until the ham is cooked.
6. Remove the ham from the liquid.
7. Remove the skin, and crush the meat with a fork, mixing the fat and the lean meat.
8. Press this mixture into a salad bowl.
9. Strain the cooking liquid, and clarify it, checking the seasoning to obtain a good colour.
10. When the liquid begins to set, add the chopped parsley, vinegar and the ¼ cup of white wine. Mix well.
11. Pour this mixture over the ham and chill.
12. The ham is usually served directly from the salad bowl.

Lapereau en Gelée au Pouilly

Rabbit in white wine aspic
From the restaurant Chez Pauline in Paris.

Serves 4

3 cups (24 fl oz) dry white burgundy wine	salt
1 large rabbit cut into pieces	pepper
3 large onions, chopped	2 tablespoons gelatine, soaked in a little cold water
1 bouquet garni	½ cup roughly chopped parsley

1. Combine the wine, pieces of rabbit, onions, bouquet garni, pepper and salt and simmer gently until the rabbit meat comes easily off the bones.
2. Remove the rabbit meat and cut it into large cubes.
3. Add the gelatine to the cooking liquid and permit it to cool.
4. Place the meat and the parsley in a terrine and pour the cooking liquid, together with the bits and pieces, over it.
5. Stir to mix all ingredients and refrigerate until set.
6. Serve cut into 2.5 cm (1 in) thick slices.

Chez Pauline, Paris.
Maître Cuisinier Paul Genin, with the help of his family, runs a typical small Parisian restaurant: cosy, unpretentious and with lots of atmosphere. They are proud of their Michelin Guide star which was awarded some 25 years ago, giving an indication of the standard of their food. Always crowded, Chez Pauline offers fine classical dishes.

Above: *A selection of dishes from Chez Pauline. Clockwise from bottom left: Jellied Ham with Parsley, Fillets of Sole (p. 116), Salmon in Champagne, Rabbit in Wine Jelly, Beef with Marrow, Foie Gras.*

Sole Normande

Normandy sole
This is not, as the name would suggest, a Normandy dish, but an Île-de-France speciality made with sole caught in Normandy.

Serves 6-8

6-8 sole (or flounder) filleted
1½ cups (12 fl oz) dry white wine
30 g (1 oz) butter
¼ cup (1 oz) flour
1 cup (8 fl oz) fish fumet (see p. 149)

125 g (4 oz) button mushrooms, sliced
salt and pepper
½ cup (4 fl oz) cream
1 dozen oysters
125 g (4 oz) peeled prawns (shrimps)

1. Poach the sole fillets in the wine for 5 minutes, or until they are just cooked.
2. Drain the fillets well, reserving the liquor. Place in a covered dish and keep warm.
3. Reduce the wine in which the fillets were cooked to approximately ½ cup.
4. In a clean saucepan, melt the butter and stir in the flour to make a roux.
5. Add the fish fumet, and then the reduced wine, stirring well with a wire whisk.
6. Season to taste with salt and pepper, and add the mushrooms. Simmer gently for 5 minutes.
7. Add the cream, oysters and prawns and cook for a few minutes longer, just until they are heated through.
8. Pour the sauce mixture over the sole fillets, and serve immediately.

Pigeon 'André Malraux'

Pigeon stuffed with livers and mushrooms
From the Restaurant Lasserre in Paris.

Serves 4

4 pigeons
salt and freshly ground black pepper

Stuffing:
100 g (3 oz) fresh lard, cut in dice
1 spring onion (scallion), chopped
thyme
bay leaf
allspice
salt and freshly ground black pepper

100 g (3 oz) mushrooms, diced, and cooked in butter
50 g (1½ oz) fresh ducks liver, diced and cooked quickly in butter
50 g (1½ oz) cockscomb, cooked and drained (optional)
100 g (3 oz) salsifis, or cucumber, diced and cooked.
butter
½ cup (4 fl oz) dry white wine
¼ cup (2 fl oz) sherry

1. Preheat the oven to 180°C (350°F).
2. Clean the pigeons and reserve their livers. Bone them by cutting down the spine, taking care to cut as little of the skin as possible, so as to make a pocket for the stuffing, and to be able to fold the skin over the opening. The drumsticks are left intact.
3. Spread the pigeons on the table, breast down, and season with salt and pepper.
4. Prepare the stuffing, by cooking the diced fresh lard in a heavy bottomed pan.
5. Add the reserved livers, spring onions, thyme, bay leaf, spice, salt and pepper, and cook over a fierce heat for a couple of minutes.
6. Add the cooked mushrooms, ducks liver, cockscomb and salsifis (or cucumber).
7. Coarsely chop this stuffing in a food processor or food mill.
8. Place about 60 g (2 oz) of this stuffing mixture in each pigeon, sewing up the opening securely.
9. Place the pigeons in a baking dish with a little butter on the top, and bake for 30 minutes.
10. When they are cooked, remove the pigeons from the baking dish, place them in a covered cocotte and keep them warm.
11. Add the white wine to the baking dish, scraping all the little pieces of pigeon together, and bring to the boil.
12. Strain, and add the sherry.
13. Pour this sauce over the pigeons and cover the cocotte.
14. Lasserre serves the pigeons with Perigord cèpes, sautéed in butter and sprinkled with herbs.

Timbale 'Élysée'

Pastry cups filled with sponge cake, ice cream and peaches
From the Restaurant Lasserre in Paris.

Serves 8

60 g (2 oz) softened butter
2 cups (8 oz) flour
1 cup (8 oz) caster (powdered) sugar
2 egg whites, stiffly beaten
1 recipe Genoise (see recipe below)
2 tablespoons Kirsch
2 cups (16 fl oz) vanilla ice cream
8 peaches, poached
3 tablespoons redcurrant syrup
1¼ cups (10 fl oz) crème chantilly
  (see recipe below)

Spun sugar domes:
125 g (4 oz) cube sugar
1 tablespoon glucose

1. Preheat the oven to 130°C (275°F).
2. Rub the butter into the flour.
3. Mix in the caster sugar.
4. Fold in the egg whites with a spatula.
5. Spread in 8 rounds, 12 to 15 cm (5-6 in) in diameter as thinly as possible on a buttered and floured baking sheet.
6. Bake for 10 to 12 minutes, or until cooked.
7. When the pastry is cool enough to handle, fit each round gently into a cup-shaped dessert glass, working quickly as the pastry loses its flexibility in minutes.
8. Make the Genoise (see recipe below).
9. When it is cool, cut it into circles to fit at the bottom of the dessert glasses.
10. Sprinkle with Kirsch.
11. Top each with a scoop of ice cream and a peach.
12. Cover with a tablespoon of redcurrant jelly.
13. Decorate with a circle of Creme Chantilly (see recipe below), using a pastry bag.
14. Each timbale should be covered with a dome of spun sugar.

Spun sugar domes

1. Boil the cube sugar, the glucose and 1 tablespoon of water until the syrup spins a very long thread or registers 150°C (310°F) on a sugar thermometer.
2. Remove from the heat.
3. Dip a fork into the syrup and pass the sugar thread to and fro across the bottom of an ungreased scoop, or ladle, working very quickly.
4. Cool and transfer to the top of the dessert glass.
5. Repeat until all the domes have been made.
6. Serve the desserts on a decorative plate, surrounded by flowers.

Génoise

4 eggs
½ cup (4 oz) sugar
½ teaspoon vanilla

2 cups (8 oz) self-raising flour, sifted
125 g (4 oz) butter, melted and cooled

1. Preheat the oven to 160°C (325°F).
2. Put the eggs, sugar and vanilla into the top of a double boiler over hot, but not boiling water.
3. Beat with a wire whisk until the mixture is thick and forms a ribbon.
4. Fold in the flour.
5. Pour in the melted butter, mixing gently with a spatula.
6. Turn the mixture into a buttered and floured pan, about 25 cm (10in) square.
7. Bake for 25 minutes.
8. Turn out on to a wire rack to cool.

Crème Chantilly

2½ cups (20 fl oz) cream
½ cup (4 oz) caster (powdered) sugar
vanilla essence

1. Beat the cream in a large chilled bowl with a wire whisk.
2. When the cream begins to thicken, beat in the sugar, little by little.
3. Add a teaspoon of vanilla if desired, and beat to a fluffy consistency.

Brittany

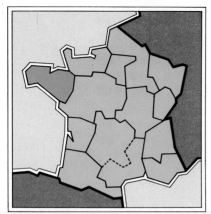

Brittany has good basic products: milk, cream and butter, and its 'salt meadow' lamb is amongst the best in the land. It is, therefore, not surprising that, although its cuisine is simple, it is wholesome and filling. À la Bretonne denotes the use of white beans, a basic peasant way of cooking (e.g. Gigot de Mouton à la Bretonne).

Being surrounded by water, many famous Breton dishes are made with seafood. In Cotriade, the local version of Bouillabaisse, butter is used instead of oil, and Homard a l'Américaine is well-known wherever good seafood is appreciated. There has always been controversy about the origins of this dish, some people believing it was invented in the south of France. But since it is often called 'à l'Armoricaine' and the Gaelic name for Brittany was Armour, it is safe to assume that this is where it originated.

Once you've tasted the dish, you won't mind much where it originated, you'll just be glad it's there.

The Breton people are hardy sailors, fishermen and industrious farmers. With the ingenuity borne out of necessity, they have created a very tasty style of cooking using simple locally available ingredients.

Local oysters are of exceptional quality and sometimes even find their way to the markets of Paris where they are eagerly bought up by gourmets.

The rivers yield plenty of pike, carp, eel, trout and even salmon and the muscadet from the south provides the perfect wine. Crêpes, which are firmly associated with French cooking in general are a Breton speciality.

One of the best known local products are the Nantes ducklings, which are highly regarded throughout France.

Brittany's windswept rock coastline doesn't contain many tourist resorts but the landscape is always picturesque and at times awe-inspiring.

Fishing boats moored at Quimper in Brittany.

Coquilles Saint-Jaques à la Marie Louise

Scallops Marie Louise
Fishing is an important industry in Brittany, and the local cooking consists largely of fish and seafood dishes.

Serves 6

24 large scallops
1 cup (8 fl oz) dry white wine
1 cup (8 fl oz) fish fumet (see page 149)
1 carrot, sliced
1 small onion, chopped
sprig of fennel
1 bay leaf
2 sprigs parsley
sprig of thyme

2 cloves
coarse salt
1 teaspoon whole peppercorns
125 g (4 oz) butter
½ cup (2 oz) flour
1 tablespoon tomato paste
4 egg yolks
¾ cup (6 fl oz) fresh cream
pinch of cayenne

1. Wash the scallops and dry them.
2. In a heavy saucepan, combine the white wine, fish fumet, carrot, onion, fennel, bay leaf, parsley, thyme, cloves, salt and peppercorns.
3. Bring to the boil, cover and simmer for 2 hours.
4. Strain through a fine sieve into a clean saucepan.
5. Add the scallops and poach very, very gently for 6 minutes. (The stock should be barely boiling, otherwise the scallops will become tough).
6. Strain, reserving the liquid.
7. Set the scallops aside, covered.
8. Heat half the butter in a heavy saucepan, add the flour and make a roux.
9. Add the scallop stock, whisking well, and the tomato paste.
10. Simmer gently for 30 minutes.
11. In the top of a double saucepan, off the heat, mix the egg yolks, the cream and the rest of the butter.
12. Add the cayenne pepper
13. Pour the hot sauce over the egg and cream mixture, whisking constantly with a wire whisk.
14. Add the scallops and heat the sauce through very briefly over boiling water.
15. Serve as soon as the scallops are hot.

Crêpes des Moines

Pancakes stuffed with seafood and coated with Aurora sauce

Serves 6

½ quantity classic pancake batter
  (see page 150)
1 tablespoon fresh tarragon, chopped,
  or 1 teaspoon of dried tarragon

Filling:
12 small rounds of lobster meat, or
6 scallops, sliced, or
30 small prawns or

18 mussels, or any combination of
  these seafoods

Sauce:
1 cup (8 fl oz) fish Velouté sauce
  (see p. 147).
1 tablespoon tomato paste
2 tablespoons fresh cream

1. Prepare the batter, add the tarragon to the batter mixture and blend well.
2. Make 12 pancakes and keep warm.
3. To make the filling, gently poach any of the seafoods which are not already cooked.
4. Make 1 cup of Velouté sauce, using fish stock and whisk in the tomato paste.
5. Add the cream, mix well and mix half of the sauce with the chosen filling.
6. Place a generous tablespoonful of the filling on each pancake, roll it up and place on an ovenproof dish.
7. When all the pancakes are filled and arranged on the dish, coat them with the remaining sauce.
8. Place them under the grill for a couple of minutes until they are a golden colour, and serve.

Homard à l'Américaine (l'Armoricaine)

Lobster à l'Américaine
There are two schools of thought about the correct name for this dish. One claims that the correct spelling should be à l'armoricaine, because armour was the old Breton name for sea, and Brittany was at one time called Armorica. The other argues that this dish could not be Breton because of its use of garlic, tomatoes and brandy, more suggestive of southern cooking.

Serves 4-6

2 live lobsters, about 1 kg (2 lb) each
125 g (4 oz) butter
½ cup (4 fl oz) olive oil
1 carrot, finely chopped
1 small onion, finely chopped
2 spring onions (scallions)
  finely chopped
2 cloves garlic, finely chopped
1 cup (8 fl oz) dry white wine
4 tablespoons brandy, warmed
1 cup (8 oz) tinned tomatoes

2 tablespoons tomato paste
1 bay leaf
½ cup (4 fl oz) fish stock, or dry
  white wine
salt and freshly ground black pepper
1 tablespoon flour
1 tablespoon butter
juice from ½ a lemon
pinch of cayenne pepper
finely chopped fresh parsley, chives
  and tarragon

1. Drop the live lobsters into warm water and bring to the boil.
2. Remove from the heat.
3. Working over a shallow bowl to catch the juices, break off and crack the claws and cut each lobster tail into thick slices.
4. Cut the body shells in half, remove and discard the intestinal tube which is exposed when the body of the lobster is cut open.
5. Reserve the coral and all the juices left in the bowl.
6. Put 3 tablespoons of butter and 3 tablespoons of oil in a heavy bottomed frying pan.
7. Gently fry the lobster pieces for 5 minutes, stirring occasionally. Reserve.
8. In another frying pan with a lid, heat the rest of the butter and oil.
9. Gently fry the chopped carrot, onion, spring onions and garlic until the onion is transparent.
10. Place the lobster pieces on top of the vegetables.
11. Pour over the wine and simmer for 3 minutes.
12. Add the warmed brandy and ignite
13. Add the tomatoes, tomato paste, bay leaf, lobster liquids, fish stock, salt and pepper to taste.
14. Cover the pan and simmer for 15 minutes.
15. Remove the lobster pieces and keep warm.
16. Cream 1 tablespoon butter with 1 tablespoon flour.
17. Blend the coral into the butter and flour.
18. Stir into the sauce and simmer until thickened.
19. Strain the sauce.
20. Flavour it to taste with lemon juice, salt, pepper and cayenne.
21. Add the lobster pieces and juice from the pan in which the lobsters were cooked, and heat through.
22. Just before serving, sprinkle with finely chopped parsley, chives and tarragon.
23. Serve with hot boiled rice.

Fricassée de Lapereau à l'Ail Doux

Fricassée of rabbit with garlic in a cream and chive sauce
From the Restaurant Ar Milin in Châteaubourg.

Serves 4

125 g (4 oz) butter
2 rabbits, boned. Only the saddle and
   thighs are used. The rest of the meat
   can be used in a ragoût, or in a pâté.

salt and freshly ground black pepper
2 cloves garlic, crushed
½ cup (4 fl oz) cream
1 bunch of chives, chopped

1. Preheat the oven to 180°C (350°F).
2. Melt half the butter in a heavy bottomed pan and brown the rabbit pieces.
3. Season with salt and pepper, and add the crushed garlic.
4. Cover the pan, and put it in the oven, allowing the rabbit to cook gently in its own steam for 1-1¼ hours. (It may be necessary to reduce the oven temperature after 15 minutes).
5. When the rabbit is cooked, melt the remaining butter in a saucepan.
6. Add the juice from the rabbit casserole, the cream and the chives.
7. Carve the saddle of rabbit into escalopes lengthwise.
8. Just before serving, cover the rabbit pieces with the sauce.
9. Serve with Pommes au Lard.

Pommes au Lard

Apples with bacon
From the Restaurant Ar Milin in Châteaubourg.

Serves 4

4 apples, peeled
4 slices streaky bacon, thinly sliced

1. Preheat the oven to 180°C (350°F).
2. Poach the peeled apples gently in water until they are only just cooked, and still firm.
3. Wrap each apple in a slice of bacon, securing with a toothpick, and place them in an ovenproof dish.
4. Cook them in the oven, without butter, until they are golden brown.
5. Serve the apples, very hot, as an accompaniment to the Fricassée of rabbit.

Breton Egg Cake

Serves 4-6

6 eggs
⅔ cup (5 oz) sugar
1½ tablespoons flour
2½ cups (20 fl oz) milk

vanilla essence
2 apples, peeled, cored and cut into
   small dice
icing (confectioners) sugar

1. Preheat the oven to 180°C (350°F).
2. Beat the eggs and sugar until they are frothy.
3. Gradually mix in the flour, milk, a few drops of vanilla essence and the apple.
4. Pour the mixture into a buttered oven dish.
5. Bake it in the oven for 40-45 minutes until the mixture has set and the top has coloured.
6. Serve hot or cold sprinkled with icing sugar.

Ar Milin, Châteaubourg.

Ar Milin is in a delightful old watermill set over the old mill stream and surrounded by a park. While its guests enjoy their food, swans glide majestically by on the pond. Chef Michel Burel's menu changes with the seasons. He uses only the best and freshest of local products and serves them in interesting traditional and regional dishes.

Above and Right: *Rabbit Fricassée with bacon-wrapped apples from Ar Milin.* **Also at Right:** *Caramelized Apple Tart (p. 129).*

Cabillaud au Four Bretonne

Baked Breton cod
Brittany is renowned for its simple, filling, country dishes, and this hearty, nourishing
treatment of the humble cod is no exception.

Serves 6

1 large onion, sliced
30 g (1 oz) butter
250 g (8 oz) bacon slices
750 g (1½ lb) potatoes, peeled and
   thinly sliced

oil
1 kg fresh cod fillets (any firm white
   fleshed fish such as snapper may
   be substituted)
salt and freshly ground black pepper
1 cup (8 fl oz) cream

1. Preheat the oven to 180°C (350°F).
2. Cook the sliced onion in 2 tablespoons of the butter.
3. Oil a deep ovenproof dish.
4. Cover the bottom with a layer of bacon slices, half the onion, and half the potato slices.
5. Place the fish, cut into medium sized pieces, on top.
6. Season well with salt and freshly ground black pepper.
7. Cover the fish with the rest of the potatoes, bacon and onions.
8. Season well and pour the cream over.
9. Dot the top with the remaining butter.
10. Cook in the oven for about 1 hour.
11. Serve from the pot in which it was cooked.

Gigot de Mouton à la Bretonne

Roast leg of mutton or lamb with white haricot beans in sauce Bretonne

Serves 6

1 leg of mutton or lamb, weighing
   about 2.5 kg (5 lb)
2 cloves garlic, slivered
sprig of thyme
bay leaves
500 g (1 lb) dried white haricot beans,
   or red kidney beans, soaked
   overnight
bouquet garni

1 onion, studded with 3 cloves
salt and pepper
30 g (1 oz) butter
6 small onions, cut in rounds
2 tablespoons consommé
1 teaspoon sugar
2 tablespoons cream
2 tablespoons Calvados (optional)

1. Preheat the oven to 200°C (400°F).
2. Trim the leg of mutton of any superfluous fat.
3. Make a few slits in the meat to hold the slivers of garlic.
4. Place the sprig of thyme and several bay leaves on top of the leg.
5. Bake in the hot oven, allowing 20 minutes per 500 g in order to have the mutton slightly pink near the bone.
6. While the meat is cooking, place the beans in a saucepan of cold water with a bouquet garni, and the onion studded with cloves. Season well.
7. Bring the beans to the boil and allow them to simmer gently until cooked, (about 1¼ hours).
8. Melt the butter in a heavy pan, and gently fry the onion rings, without letting them take on any colour.
9. Add the consommé, and bring to the boil. Simmer for 5 minutes.
10. Remove the pan from the heat and add the sugar and cream.
11. When the beans are cooked, drain them well.
12. Pour the sauce over the beans, stir gently and place in a warmed serving dish.
13. Just before serving the mutton, pour the 2 tablespoons of Calvados over the meat, and serve the beans separately.

Tarte aux Pommes Caramelisées

Caramelised apple tart
From the Restaurant Ar Milin in Châteaubourg.

Serves 4

Filling:
30 g (1 oz) butter
⅓ cup (3 oz) sugar
5 apples, peeled, cored, and sliced
 in rounds

Pastry:
155 g (5 oz) butter
2 cups (8 oz) flour
pinch of salt
1 egg

1. Preheat the oven to 180°C (350°F).
2. Butter the bottom of a teflon coated pie dish.
3. Sprinkle with the sugar.
4. Arrange the apples on the sugar, overlapping them slightly.
5. Prepare the pastry by rubbing the butter into the flour and salt.
6. Bind with the egg, and a little cold water if necessary.
7. Roll out thinly and cut a round to cover the pie dish.
8. Place the pie in the oven for approximately 25 minutes.
9. When the tart is cooked, place the pie on a hot plate until the apples are well caramelised.
10. Allow the pie to cool.
11. Turn the pie out on to a serving dish.
12. Serve with whipped cream.

Gâteau Breton

Breton cake
This is a thick galette flavoured with rum.

Serves 10

2¼ cups (9 oz) flour
1 cup (7 oz) sugar
pinch of salt

250 g (8 oz) unsalted butter, softened
6 egg yolks
2 tablespoons rum

1. Preheat the oven to 180°C (350°F).
2. Place 1¾ cups flour in a bowl and make a well in the centre.
3. Put into the well the sugar, salt, butter, 5 egg yolks and the rum.
4. Mix and then work well together as if for short crust pastry.
5. Add the rest of the flour.
6. Form the dough into a ball with your hands.
7. Butter a 23 cm (9 in) cake tin.
8. Roll out the dough to a thickness of about 3 cm (1¼ in).
9. Line the tin with the dough.
10. Dilute the remaining egg yolk with a drop of water, and brush over the cake.
11. Make a criss cross pattern on the top of the cake with a fork.
12. Bake for about 20 minutes, or until it is golden.

Normandy

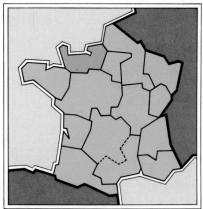

In most parts of France, good wine goes hand-in-hand with good food.

This region produces no wine, yet in Normandy a quality cuisine has developed. Apple juice, cider and Calvados (distilled from apple juice) seem hardly inspiring enough to influence the regional cooking, yet a great number of excellent dishes make use of these local ingredients. Probably best-known for its dairy products, Normandy milk, cream and butter are the best in France.

The country is rich in beef, cattle and lamb too. In addition to apples, the orchards grow other high-quality fruit. Rivers yield trout and salmon, while the ocean supplies sole, flounder, mussels, shrimps and oysters.

No wonder then that Normandy cooking enjoys such a high reputation among the provinces of France.

Tripes à la Mode de Caen would not be the same without cider and the Soufflé Normandy demonstrates the great flavour that Calvados imparts. 'À la Normande' when applied to the preparation of cuts of meat and chicken means that cider and Calvados are used to enrich the flavour of the dish.

Many Normandy specialities are cooked with cream or 'graisse normande', a mixture of equal parts of melted down pork fat and suet, flavoured with vegetables and herbs and seasoned with salt and pepper.

Among the seafood dishes of Normandy, Sole à la Normande is most famous and combines two regional products: sole and Normandy cream, while in the Matelot à la Normande, the saltwater fish is combined with milk, cream, cider and Calvados.

Omelettes are a speciality of the region and being dairy country local cheeses are household names; Camembert, Pont l'Evêque and Gervais Petit Suisse.

In addition to being a gourmet's delight, Normandy is very popular for summer vacations. Many families spend farmhouse holidays in the Normandy countryside, particularly in early autumn when the orchards are laden with ripe fruit. In summer, it is the Channel Coast which attracts most holiday makers who spend their time swimming and sunbaking along the beaches.

One of the most striking monuments, not only in Normandy, but in the whole of France, is Mt. St. Michel, that unusual peak in the middle of the tidal flats in the south-western corner of the region. It is interesting to note that while it is surrounded by water, except for a causeway, at low tide no water can be seen anywhere from Mt. St. Michel.

It is here that the low salty meadows of the coastline produce that famous salt meadow mutton, so highly regarded by French gourmets.

Village church in Normandy.

Beignets d'Huîtres à la Normande

Oyster fritters

Serves 6

1 cup (8 fl oz) dry white wine
1 cup (8 fl oz) water
3 dozen oysters, shelled
1 cup (8 fl oz) fish Velouté
  (see page 147)

Batter:
1¼ cups (5 oz) flour
⅓ cup (2½ fl oz) water
⅓ cup (2½ fl oz) milk
salt
2 eggs, separated
½ tablespoon oil
oil for deep frying

1. Bring the wine and water to the boil with the salt and pepper.
2. Gently poach the oysters for 2 minutes.
3. Drain and dry the oysters well, reserving the liquid.
4. Prepare the fish Velouté sauce.
5. Prepare the batter mixture by mixing the flour, water, milk, salt, egg yolks and oil together.
6. Beat the egg whites until they are stiff.
7. Fold the egg whites into the batter mixture.
8. Add 4 tablespoons of the oyster liquid to the fish Velouté sauce, so that it just coats the back of the spoon.
9. Heat the deep frying oil until it is very hot.
10. Dip the well dried oysters in the sauce one by one.
11. Dip them in the batter and deep fry them a few at a time over a hot heat until the fritters have swelled and are a fine golden colour.
12. Drain them well and keep warm until all the oysters have been cooked.
13. Serve them hot.

Potage Velouté de Crevettes à la Normande

Cream of prawn soup, Normandy style

Serves 6

500 g (1 lb) cooked school prawns
  (shrimps), shelled
5 cups (1.25 litres) fish fumet
  (see page 149)
90 g (3 oz) butter

¾ cup (3 oz) flour
3 egg yolks
½ cup (4 fl oz) cream
12 oysters
salt and pepper

1. Prepare the fish fumet, using the prawn shells. Strain.
2. In a large saucepan, melt the butter and add the flour to make a roux.
3. Whisking well all the time, add the fish fumet to the roux to make a Velouté sauce. Season well.
4. Pound ¾ of the prawns in a mortar, or process them lightly in a food processor.
5. Add the pounded prawns to the fish Velouté, and simmer gently for 5 minutes.
6. In a bowl, whisk the egg yolks and the cream together.
7. Whisking continuously, beat the Velouté sauce into the egg and cream mixture.
8. Return this mixture to the saucepan.
9. Add the rest of the prawns and the oysters to the soup.
10. Heat the soup through, stirring well, taking care not to let it boil, and serve.

Poulet Sauté Vallée d'Auge

Sautéed chicken with Calvados and cream sauce

Serves 4

1.5 kg (3 lb) chicken, jointed
90 g (3 oz) butter
2 tablespoons oil
salt and pepper
⅓ cup (2½ fl oz) Calvados
½ cup (4 fl oz) chicken stock
1 spring onion (scallion),
  finely chopped

1 stalk celery, finely chopped
185 g (6 oz) tart apples, peeled,
  cored and coarsely chopped
1 teaspoon dried thyme
2 egg yolks
½ cup (4 fl oz) cream
watercress or parsley sprigs

1. Melt 60 g of the butter and the oil in a heavy frying pan and brown the chicken on all sides.
2. Pour off all but a thin film of fat, return the chicken to the pan and add salt and pepper.
3. Warm the Calvados in a small saucepan and ignite it.
4. Pour it over the chicken, a little at a time, shaking the pan gently until the flame dies.
5. Add the chicken stock, and scrape any brown bits clinging to the pan.
6. In a clean frying pan, melt the remaining butter, and cook the spring onions, celery, apples and thyme for 10 minutes, stirring from time to time, until they are soft, but not browned.
7. Spread the vegetable and fruit mixture over the chicken pieces. Return the frying pan with the chicken to a high heat and bring the stock to the boil.
8. Cover the pan, reduce the heat and simmer the chicken for 15 minutes, basting occasionally.
9. When the chicken is tender, remove the pieces from the pan, and arrange on a large warmed dish. Cover the chicken with foil and keep it warm in a low oven.
10. Strain the contents of the frying pan through a fine sieve into a small saucepan, pressing down well. Skim off as much of the surface fat as possible.
11. Bring this sauce to the boil over a high heat, and cook until it is reduced to about ½ a cup.
12. Blend the egg yolks and the cream in a bowl with a wire whisk. Gradually beat in all the hot sauce, whisking well.
13. Pour back into saucepan and cook over a gentle heat, whisking constantly until the sauce thickens. Never allow the sauce to boil or it will curdle. Taste and correct the seasoning.
14. To serve, cover each piece of the chicken with the sauce, and decorate with small bunches of watercress or parsley.

Tripes à la Mode de Caen

Tripe as prepared in Caen is one of the most famous of all Normandy dishes, the secret of which is very long, slow cooking in a tightly sealed heavy casserole dish.

Serves 4-6

1 kg (2 lb) tripe
1 calf's foot
125 g (4 oz) fat bacon
2 medium carrots, chopped in rounds
2 medium onions, coarsely chopped

bouquet garni
cloves
salt and pepper
pinch of cayenne pepper
4 cups (1 litre) cider

1. Heat the oven to 160°C (325°F).
2. Simmer the tripe in salted water for ½ hour, drain. Cut it into large squares.
3. Bone the calf's foot, and dice the meat from it.
4. Line a heavy casserole dish with a well fitting lid with slices of fat bacon.
5. Place the chopped vegetables on top of the bacon, then the bones of the calf's foot, and all the seasoning.
6. Lay the tripe and meat from the calf's foot on top and cover with the cider.
7. Cook in the oven for ½ hour.
8. Reduce the oven temperature to 120°C (250°F), and cook for about 7½ hours, reducing the oven temperature still further if the casserole dish appears to steam.
9. Serve the tripe with the liquid in deep plates, such as old fashioned soup plates.

La Panachée de la Criée

Mixed seafood salad
From the Restaurant Joignant in Caen.

Serves 4

250 g (8 oz) French beans,
lightly cooked
4 tomatoes, finely sliced
4 eggs, hard-boiled and cut in half
3 small carrots, blanched and sliced
250 g (8 oz) prawns (shrimp), peeled
8 king prawns, or 1 small lobster, cut
into medallions
lettuce, shredded

Vinaigrette dressing
½ cup (4 fl oz) olive oil
1½ tablespoons vinegar, or
lemon juice
1 good teaspoon mustard
salt and freshly ground black pepper

1. On a serving dish make a bed of shredded lettuce.
2. Arrange the vegetables, eggs and seafood decoratively on the top.
3. Just before serving, blend all the ingredients for the dressing, and pour over the top.

Daurade aux Concombres

Daurade with cucumbers (since Daurade is unobtainable here, any firm fleshed fish, such as snapper fillets may be substituted)
This recipe comes from the Restaurant Joignant in Caen.

Serves 4

2 onions, finely chopped
2 small green peppers, finely chopped
2 small red peppers, finely chopped
olive oil

2 snapper, filleted
1¼ cups (10 fl oz) Calvados
2 cucumbers, finely sliced
1¼ cups (10 fl oz) cream

1. Preheat the oven to 180°C (350°F).
2. Soften the onions and peppers in a little oil for a few minutes.
3. Transfer these to a large shallow ovenproof dish.
4. Arrange the fish fillets on top of this bed of vegetables, and moisten with a few drops of olive oil.
5. Cook in the oven for 10 minutes.
6. Strain off the liquid resulting from the cooking of the fish and reserve.
7. In a clean pan, flame the fish fillets with the Calvados, and allow the flames to die out.
8. Pour off any resulting juice, and add to the liquid already reserved.
9. Rearrange the fish fillets in the ovenproof dish on top of the vegetables and cover them with the finely sliced cucumbers.
10. Return the dish to the oven for a further 10 minutes.
11. Heat the reserved liquid, and add the cream.
12. Correct the seasoning.
13. When ready to serve, pour the sauce over the fish fillets.

Restaurant Joignant, Caen.

Maître Cuisinier Claude's most well-known speciality is Les Tripes à la Mode de Caen. It's one of the most famous dishes from the Normandy cuisine and the Joignant is the best place to try it. Claude also offers some fine seafood fresh from the nearby Channel and many dishes which incorporate the great products of the region: cream, cider and Calvados. No meal at Joignant would be complete without some of the local cheeses: Camembert, Livarot and Pont l'Evêque.

Above: *A selection of food from the Restaurant Joignant in Caen. Clockwise from bottom left: Fish with Cucumbers, Mixed Seafood Salad, Veal with Maize flour Pancakes (p. 136).*

Grenadins de Veau des Bords de la Dives

Escalopes of Veal with maize flour pancakes
From the Restaurant Joignant in Caen.

Serves 4

4 veal escalopes, trimmed
flour
butter
1 onion, finely chopped
¼ cup (2 fl oz) sherry

1¼ cups (10 fl oz) fresh cream
2 eggs
200 g (6 oz) maize flour
salt and freshly ground black pepper

1. Dust the veal escalopes with a little flour.
2. Melt a knob of butter in a heavy bottomed pan, and brown the escalopes on both sides. Remove and keep warm.
3. Melt a little more butter in the pan, and cook the onion gently until it is soft and golden.
4. Add the sherry, and stir the pan well.
5. Allow to cool a little, before adding half the cream.
6. Adjust the seasoning, adding salt and pepper as necessary.
7. Meanwhile, in a bowl, beat together the eggs and remaining cream.
8. Slowly add the maize flour and a little salt, beating well to make a batter.
9. Take a pancake pan and moisten with a little butter.
10. Proceed to make small pancakes with the batter in the usual way.
11. Heat the sauce through, and serve each escalope with a little sauce over the top, accompanied by a pancake.

Sole à la Normande

The real Normandy sole prepared in the local way combines the abundance of the sea with the excellent heavy cream produced in Normandy. Flounder or John Dory may be substituted if sole is not available.

Serves 6

6 sole each weighing about 310 g (10 oz)
¾ cup (6 fl oz) dry white wine
sprig of thyme
sprig of parsley
1 bay leaf
1 stalk of celery, chopped
1 teaspooon whole white peppercorns
1 cup (8 fl oz) water
salt

Sauce:
90 g (3 oz) butter
18 oysters or 30 mussels
125 g (4 oz) tiny prawns (shrimps) shelled
90 g (3 oz) button mushrooms
½ cup (2 oz) flour
⅔ cup (5 fl oz) cream
pinch of cayenne pepper

1. Have the soles filleted.
2. Put all the trimmings, heads, bones, fins and skin, into a heavy saucepan with the wine, thyme, parsley, bay leaf, celery and peppercorns.
3. Add the water and salt and simmer, partly covered, for 30 minutes.
4. Strain this stock into a shallow pan.
5. Poach the fillets in this stock very gently for 10 to 15 minutes.
6. Heat 30 g of the butter in a heavy frying pan and sauté the oysters or mussels, the prawns and mushrooms.
7. Remove the fillets from the poaching liquid, and arrange on a heated serving dish. Reserve the stock.
8. Garnish with the oysters, prawns and mushrooms, and keep warm.
9. In a clean saucepan, melt the rest of the butter and add the flour to make a roux.
10. Little by little, whisking constantly, add the stock. Cook very gently for 15 minutes.
11. Stir in the cream.
12. Adjust the seasoning and add the cayenne pepper.
13. Pour the sauce over the sole fillets.
14. Glaze the surface by placing the dish under the grill until it is golden brown. Serve.

Bourdelots Normands

Normandy apples cooked in a crust

Serves 6

750 g (1½ lb) flaky pastry
6 tart apples
⅓ cup (2 oz) raisins
cinnamon

⅓ cup (2 oz) brown sugar
mixed spice
milk
caster (powdered) sugar

1. Heat the oven to 160°C (325°F).
2. Prepare the pastry.
3. Core the apples.
4. Roll out the pastry until quite thin.
5. Place an apple on the pastry, well in from the edge.
6. Mix the raisins, cinnamon, sugar and a pinch of mixed spice, and stuff the apple with this mixture.
7. Cut round the apple, leaving a margin of pastry to fold over.
8. Fold the pastry over the top of the fruit, dampen the edges with milk and press together.
9. Repeat this process with each apple.
10. Brush the pastry with a little milk.
11. Place on a buttered dish and bake in the oven for 30 minutes, or until the pastry is cooked.
12. Dust with caster sugar and serve either hot or cold.

Soufflé Normande

Apple Soufflé
This is flavoured with Calvados, and stuffed with macaroons and pieces of cooked apples.

Serves 4-6

60 g (2 oz) butter
½ cup (2 oz) flour
1¼ cups (10 fl oz) hot milk
pinch of salt
5 egg yolks
½ cup (4 oz) sugar
½ teaspoon vanilla essence

3 tablespoons Calvados
½ large apple, peeled, chopped into
**   small pieces and cooked in water**
**   until tender**
6 egg whites
6 macaroons

1. Preheat the oven to 180°C (350°F).
2. Melt the butter in the top of a double saucepan.
3. Add the flour and cook, stirring, until well blended.
4. Add the hot milk, and salt.
5. Cook the sauce, stirring constantly, until smooth and thick.
6. Let the sauce cool slightly.
7. Beat the egg yolks with the sugar and the vanilla essence, and mix well with the cooled sauce.
8. Stir in 2 tablespoons Calvados and the cooked apple pieces.
9. Line a buttered soufflé dish with the macaroons.
10. Sprinkle them with the remaining tablespoon of Calvados.
11. Beat the egg whites until stiff, but not dry.
12. Fold the egg whites into the cooled sauce mixture.
13. Pour into the prepared soufflé dish.
14. Bake in the centre of the oven for 35 minutes, or until the soufflé is puffed and golden.
15. Serve immediately.

Champagne, Picardy, Artois, Flanders

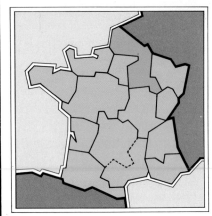

When thinking about the region of Champagne it is easier to talk about its wines than about regional food. It is indeed the only area in France producing great wines which has not developed a correspondingly good cuisine.

Someone has suggested that this may be due to the fact that champagne is produced so laboriously and at such great expense that it is not used in cooking. This may be true and also there is the fact that the sparkling effect is soon lost in cooking.

The region does produce some non-sparkling wines of a very respectable quality but somehow even those are not sufficiently inspiring to foster the development of a distinctive cuisine.

That is not to say there is no good regional food: the charcuterie products are of good quality, poultry-breeding is quite extensive and in some parts chicken in champagne is a truly local speciality. So is champagne sauce for the trout and salmon from the local rivers.

But in general, most dishes prepared in the province have originated in other areas. Burgundy to the south and Lorraine to the east have contributed to the cooking of Champagne. One can also see the influence of the Île-de-France or even the Touraine.

To the north, linked by a short border to the Champagne region, are Picardy, Artois and Flanders.

These are the northern flatlands which make a very modest contribution towards the overall picture of the French regional cuisine.

One would imagine that Picardy with its coastline along the channel would have a considerable range of seafood specialities, but only a few exist. Its best regional product is 'salty mutton' from the salty meadows along the coast.

Tripe, sausage and tripe soup are of Normandy origin but in the Picardy version of the soup, pig's offal is used. Cachuse (fresh pork braised with onions) is very much a local dish and the duck pâté of Amiens is tasty.

Artois, with its changing history does not have many well-established culinary traditions. Its cooking uses good local products: excellent vegetables, good beef and mutton and from its rivers, trout and salmon.

To quote an authority, the cooking of Artois is 'foreign cuisine naturalised in France'.

The Flanders region, despite its short coastline, has many seafood specialities. For example, herrings are prepared in many ways: Harengs salés and fumés or Harengs Kippers.

Its beer soup is of German origin and many other dishes show Flemish influence.

Vineyard in Champagne area.

138

Soupe à la Bière
Beer soup

Serves 6

60 g (2 oz) butter
½ cup (2 oz) flour
6 cups (1.5 litres) light beer
salt and pepper

pinch of cinnamon
1 teaspoon of sugar
¾ cup (6 fl oz) cream
slices of toast

1. Melt the butter, and stir in the flour to make a roux.
2. Whisk in the beer, stirring well.
3. Season to taste with salt, pepper and cinnamon.
4. Bring to the boil and add the sugar.
5. Blend in the cream and pour over slices of toast.

Soupe à la Bonne Femme
Leek and potato soup

Serves 6-8

4 leeks, the white parts only,
   finely shredded
125 g (4 oz) butter
8 cups (2 litres) chicken stock

375 g (12 oz) potatoes, cut in
   thin slices
salt and pepper
1 tablespoon chopped fresh
   chervil leaves

1. Cook the leeks in a covered saucepan in half the butter, without allowing the leeks to colour.
2. When the leeks are cooked and quite soft, add the stock and bring to the boil.
3. Add the potatoes.
4. Bring to the boil, reduce the heat and simmer gently. Check the seasoning.
5. At the last moment, when the poatoes are just cooked through, remove the saucepan from the heat and add the rest of the butter and the chervil leaves.

Le Poulet au Champagne d'Épernay
Chicken in champagne

Serves 4

250 g (8 oz) butter
1.5 kg (3 lb) chicken, quartered
½ cup (4 fl oz) brandy
2 cups (16 fl oz) dry Champagne

½ cup (4 fl oz) veal or chicken stock
5 tablespoons cream
1 teaspoon tomato paste
salt and freshly ground black pepper

1. Heat half the butter in a heavy pan.
2. Sauté the chicken pieces gently for half an hour without letting them take on any colour.
3. Heat the brandy, ignite it and pour it over the chicken.
4. Add the champagne and the stock.
5. Cover the pan and simmer gently for a further half an hour.
6. Remove the chicken pieces to a serving dish and keep them warm.
7. Reduce the liquid in the pan to half.
8. Add the cream and cook until the sauce is slightly thickened.
9. Add the tomato paste to colour the sauce.
10. Beat in the rest of the butter, using a wire whisk.
11. Adjust the seasoning and pour the sauce over the chicken.

Truite à la Champenoise

Trout in champagne sauce

Serves 6

6 trout each weighing about 250 g
  (8 oz)
salt and freshly ground black pepper
2 medium sized onions, finely sliced
bouquet garni

1½ cups (12 fl oz) Champagne
125 g (4 oz) butter
½ cup (2 oz) flour
2 egg yolks

1. Season the trout inside and out with salt and pepper.
2. Place in a buttered dish with the onions and a bouquet garni.
3. Moisten with ½ cup of champagne.
4. Cover and simmer for 10 to 15 minutes until the trout is just cooked.
5. Drain the trout and arrange on a warmed serving dish.
6. In a clean saucepan, melt half the butter and add the flour, stirring well to make a roux.
7. Strain the fish liquid into the roux, whisking well, and then add the rest of the champagne.
8. Bring the sauce to the boil and simmer for two minutes, whisking all the time.
9. Add the egg yolks, beating well.
10. Little by little incorporate the rest of the butter into the sauce, beating all the time.
11. Correct the seasoning, glaze the trout with the sauce under a hot grill and serve.

Hochepot

Flemish hotpot
*A hearty peasant dish, much favoured in the cold weather, served with onion sauce, boiled
potatoes and cabbage.*

Serves 8

500 g (1 lb) boneless shoulder of lamb
500 g (1 lb) salted topside (the butcher
  will salt it for you)
500 g (1 lb) lean salt pork
500 g (1 lb) streaky bacon, in
  one piece
250 g (8 oz) carrots, small
250 g (8 oz) onions, small
4 leeks, trimmed and cleaned
4 turnips, medium sized
1 large parsnip, quartered
bouquet garni
salt and pepper
juniper berries

Onion Sauce:
2 cups (16 fl oz) Béchamel sauce
  (see p. 147)
125 g (4 oz) onions, finely chopped
salt and pepper
1 tablespoon white wine vinegar

1. Place all the different pieces of meat into a large saucepan. Cover with cold water and bring to the boil.
2. Skim the saucepan well.
3. Add the whole vegetables, and the bouquet garni, and season well.
4. Add a few crushed juniper berries.
5. Reduce the heat and simmer gently until all the meats are cooked.
6. Each piece of meat takes a different length of time to cook. For the lamb, allow 20 minutes per 500 g plus 20 minutes. For the beef and pork allow 25 minutes per 500 g plus 25 minutes.
7. As each is cooked, remove it from the liquid and keep warm on a covered serving dish, to prevent it from drying out.
8. Arrange the vegetables around the meats, and serve accompanied by onion sauce, boiled potatoes and cabbage.

Onion Sauce
1. While the meats are cooking, prepare 2 cups of Béchamel sauce.
2. Add the onions to the Béchamel.
3. Season well with salt and freshly ground black pepper.
4. Add the vinegar and stir well.
5. Simmer gently for 1 hour and serve with the hochepot.

Escalope de Saumon au Citron Vert et Gingembre

Escalopes of salmon with lime and ginger
If salmon is unobtainable, substitute a large trout. This recipe comes from the Restaurant La Chaumière in Reims.

Serves 6

750 g (1½ lb) salmon, cut into
   12 escalopes about 1.5-2 cm (¾ in)
   thick
salt and freshly ground black pepper
4 limes, cut in slices
finely grated rind of 1 lemon
chervil
a few thin strips of fresh root ginger

Sauce:
1 cup (8 fl oz) white port
½ cup (4 fl oz) lemon juice
1¼ cups (10 fl oz) cream
155 g (5 oz) butter
a few thin strips of fresh root ginger
salt and freshly ground black pepper

1. Preheat the oven to 250°C (475°F).
2. Cut two circles of silver foil about 30 cm (12 in) in diameter.
3. Fold each circle in two.
4. Place 6 salmon escalopes on one half of each foil circle.
5. Season them lightly with salt and pepper.
6. Place 3 slices of lime on each escalope, a little lemon rind, some chervil and a julienne strip of ginger.
7. Fold the top half of the foil over the top of the salmon and pinch the edges together to make a good seal.
8. Cook in the hot oven for 6-7 minutes.
9. To make the sauce, combine the port and lemon juice in a saucepan, and boil vigorously until it is reduced by half.
10. Add the cream and reduce again by half.
11. Using a wire whisk, blend in the butter, beating well.
12. Add a few strips of ginger to taste.
13. Correct the seasoning and strain through a fine sieve.
14. To serve, open the foil with a sharp knife. On each well heated plate, pour three tablespoons of sauce, and arrange 2 salmon escalopes on top.

Gougère de l'Aube

Cheese and egg pastry
This may be eaten either hot or cold.

Serves 6-8

1 cup (8 fl oz) water
125 g (4 oz) butter
1 teaspoon salt
1½ cups (6 oz) flour

6 eggs
125 g (4 oz) Gruyère cheese,
   finely diced
pinch of white pepper

1. Heat the oven to 180°C (350°F).
2. In a heavy saucepan combine the water, butter and salt, and bring to the boil.
3. Remove the saucepan from the heat and add the flour.
4. Mix, then dry the dough over a light heat, stirring with a wooden spoon until it comes away from the sides of the saucepan easily.
5. Remove the saucepan from the heat and beat 5 of the eggs into the mixture, one by one.
6. Add all but 1 tablespoon of the cheese and the pepper and mix well.
7. With a tablespoon, scoop out pieces of dough, each the size of an egg, and put them straight into a buttered pie dish, one against the other in a circle.
8. Smooth the circle on top and round the inside with the back of a spoon.
9. Brush with the remaining beaten egg.
10. Sprinkle with the remaining tablespoon of cheese.
11. Bake for about 30 minutes. The Gougère is cooked when it is brittle on the surface.

La Chaumière, Reims.
The modest exterior of La Chaumière hides a pleasant surprise: a very elegant interior and also some of the best food in France. Good enough in fact to have been awarded three Michelin Guide stars. Gaston Boyer and his son Gérard use fresh seasonal produce to prepare original dishes of exceptional quality. Their three stars are well deserved.

Above: *Salmon with lime and ginger from La Chaumière in Reims.*

Côtes de Porc Avesnoise

Pork Chops Avesnes style

Serves 6

60 g (2 oz) butter
6 pork chops
salt and freshly ground black pepper
125 g (4 oz) grated Gruyère cheese

4 tablespoons cream
4 tablespoons mustard
2 tablespoons Calvados

1. Heat the butter in a heavy bottomed pan, and fry the chops on both sides until they are done (15 to 20 minutes).
2. Remove the chops to an ovenproof dish, season with salt and pepper and keep them warm.
3. Mix together the Gruyère cheese, 2 tablespoons of the cream, and the mustard.
4. Spread the mixture on the chops, and place under the grill until they are richly coloured.
5. Keep the chops warm while preparing the sauce.
6. Pour the Calvados into the frying pan and add the remaining two tablespoons of cream.
7. Reduce over a brisk flame until the sauce is thick.
8. Correct the seasoning, pour over the chops and serve.

Côtes de Veau à l'Ardennaise

Braised veal chops with ham and parsley dressing

Serves 6

125 g (4 oz) butter
2 onions, finely chopped
1 carrot, finely chopped
10 juniper berries
½ teaspoon dried basil
½ teaspoon salt
freshly ground black pepper
6 veal chops

3 tablespoons oil
1 cup (8 fl oz) dry white wine
½ cup (4 fl oz) chicken stock
¾ cup (1½ oz) fresh white
   breadcrumbs
1 tablespoon finely chopped ham
2 tablespoons parsley, finely chopped
1 teaspoon lemon juice

1. Preheat the oven to 180°C (350°F).
2. Take a large shallow flameproof casserole with a lid (one that is large enough to take the chops in one layer) and melt 30 g of the butter in it.
3. Cook the chopped onions and carrot for 5 minutes until they are slightly coloured. Set aside.
4. With a mortar and pestle, crush the juniper berries, the basil, salt and pepper.
5. Press this seasoning into both sides of the chops, forcing it into the meat as much as possible.
6. In a heavy frying pan, melt 30 g of butter and the oil.
7. Brown the chops on both sides, turning carefully only once, so as not to dislodge the seasoning. Transfer the chops to the casserole.
8. Pour off almost all the fat from the frying pan, and add the wine. Boil briskly, scraping the pan well, until the wine is reduced to ½ a cup.
9. Stir in the stock and pour the mixture round the chops carefully.
10. In a clean frying pan, melt all but 1 tablespoon of the remaining butter and cook the breadcrumbs until they are lightly browned. Remove from the heat.
11. Stir in the ham, parsley and lemon juice.
12. Spoon a portion of the mixture on to each chop and dot the topping with the remaining butter.
13. Bring the casserole to a boil on top of the stove, cover tightly and bake for approximately 30 minutes.
14. When the chops are cooked, transfer them to a heated dish.
15. Strain the contents of the casserole into a small saucepan, pressing the vegetables hard with the back of a spoon.
16. Boil down the liquid over a high heat until they are reduced to about ½ a cup.
17. Correct the seasoning, pour around the chops and serve.

Coq au Vin de Bouzy

Chicken cooked in Bouzy wine
Bouzy is a red wine from the Champagne district, and this tasty dish is the local version of coq au vin.

Serves 4

125 g (4 oz) butter
1.75 kg (3½ lb) chicken, jointed
2 medium onions, chopped
2 small carrots, finely chopped
salt and freshly ground black pepper
1 bottle dry red wine
1 tablespoon cornflour (cornstarch)
1 tablespoon brandy

310 g (10 oz) artichoke hearts, diced
125 g (4 oz) salt pork, diced and fried
125 g (4 oz) button mushrooms
125 g (4 oz) cocktail sausages, diced
125 g (4 oz) tripe, boiled, drained and
  diced (optional)
1 cup (4 oz) croûtons

1. Melt half the butter in a large, heavy casserole dish, add the chicken pieces, onions and carrots and sauté for 10 minutes, or until the chicken pieces are golden on both sides.
2. Season to taste with salt and pepper.
3. Add the wine and cook over a low heat for 35 minutes.
4. Remove the chicken pieces to a serving dish and keep them warm.
5. Reduce the liquid in the casserole to half its original volume.
6. Dissolve the cornflour in a little water.
7. Add the cornflour to the casserole and cook, stirring until the sauce has thickened.
8. Add half the remaining butter and the brandy.
9. Stir in the artichoke hearts, salt pork, mushrooms, cocktail sausages and tripe. Heat through.
10. In a clean frying pan melt the remaining butter and fry the croûtons until crisp.
11. Pour the sauce over the chicken, and serve the croûtons separately.

Lapin de Garenne aux Pruneaux

Rabbit with prunes in cider sauce

Serves 6

185 g (6 oz) prunes, stoned
3 cups (24 fl oz) dry cider
6 rabbit joints (hindquarters and
  saddle pieces)
200 g (6½ oz) butter

500 g (1 lb) spring onions (scallions)
  finely chopped
fresh thyme
salt and freshly ground black pepper
6 tablespoons Calvados, warmed

1. Marinate the prunes in the cider for several hours. Drain.
2. Wipe the rabbit joints.
3. Melt half the butter in a flameproof casserole dish and fry the rabbit pieces until evenly browned on all sides.
4. Add the spring onions and the thyme and cook gently, until the spring onions are soft, but not browned.
5. Season with salt and freshly ground black pepper.
6. Pour in the warmed Calvados and ignite.
7. When the flames have died down, pour in the cider and simmer, very gently, without a cover, until the rabbit is very tender (about 45 minutes).
8. While the rabbit is cooking, sauté the prunes gently in the rest of the butter, taking care to keep turning them so that they do not burn.
9. When the rabbit is cooked, transfer the pieces to a serving dish with the prunes and keep warm.
10. Increase the heat under the casserole dish and reduce the liquid in which the rabbit has been cooking until it is a rich consistency.
11. Correct the seasoning.
12. Pour over the rabbit pieces and the prunes and serve.

Restaurant Le Champenoise, Audresselles.
Chef Lucien Fleury (above) runs a modest little place along the windswept, almost barren Channel coastline, halfway between Boulogne and Calais.
His speciality is his own invention, a type of seafood fondue: pieces of fish, scallops, prawns, mussels and cuttlefish cooked at the table in hot oil and then dipped into a choice of 3 delicious sauces: Sauce l'Américaine (fish stock, tomatoes and wine); Sauce l'Audressellaise (cream and tomato); and Sauce la Champenoise (fish stock, Champagne and cream).

Above: *Ingredients for Le Champenoise' famous seafood fondue.*

Béchamel Sauce

White sauce

Makes 2 cups (16 fl oz)

2 cups (16 fl oz) milk
½ bay leaf
sprig of thyme
1 small onion, peeled

pinch of nutmeg
60 g (2 oz) butter
½ cup (2 oz) flour
salt and pepper

1. Bring the milk to the boil with the bay leaf, thyme, onion and nutmeg.
2. Remove the mixture from the heat and leave it to infuse for 15 minutes.
3. In a clean saucepan melt the butter, add the flour and stir well to make a roux.
4. Strain the milk into the roux, whisking well all the time until it is thick and creamy.
5. Allow to simmer gently for 3 minutes, stirring constantly, to dissipate any taste of flour.
6. Add salt and pepper to taste.

Velouté Sauce

Makes 2½ cups (20 fl oz)

60 g (2 oz) butter
½ cup (2 oz) flour
2½ cups (20 fl oz) white stock
(may be chicken, veal, or fish for a
fish Velouté)

salt and white pepper
4 small mushrooms, wiped clean and
thinly sliced (optional)

1. Melt the butter in a heavy saucepan.
2. Add the flour and cook, stirring constantly, for a few minutes to form a roux.
3. Add the boiling stock, salt and pepper, and cook for 2 minutes, stirring constantly with a wire whisk.
4. Add the mushrooms, and cook slowly, stirring occasionally.
5. When the sauce is thick, yet light and creamy, it is ready.
6. Strain through a fine sieve.

Sauce Béarnaise

Makes approximately 1½ cups (12 fl oz)

1 teaspoon dried tarragon
2 teaspoons dried chervil
1 tablespoon chopped spring onions
(scallions)
2 peppercorns, crushed
2 tablespoons white wine vinegar

⅔ cup (5 fl oz) dry white wine
3 egg yolks
1 tablespoon water
250 g (8 oz) soft butter, cut into
small pieces
salt and pepper

1. Combine the tarragon, chervil, spring onions, peppercorns, vinegar and white wine in a saucepan.
2. Cook the liquid over a high heat until it is reduced to half its original quantity.
3. Place the egg yolks, herb and wine mixture and water in the top of a double saucepan over hot but not boiling water, and stir briskly with a wire whisk until it is light and fluffy.
4. Never let the water in the bottom of the saucepan boil or the sauce will curdle.
5. Add the butter, piece by piece, to the egg mixture, stirring briskly all the time as the sauce begins to thicken.
6. Season to taste with salt and pepper.
7. Strain through a fine sieve and serve.

Brown Meat Stock

Meat stock is very useful in the preparation of soups and sauces; the quantity given here may seem excessive, but it can be deep frozen and kept at hand for future use.

Makes 16 cups (4 litres)

2 kg (4 lb) shin beef on the bone
2 kg (4 lb) veal knuckle (cut into 5 cm
 (2 in) pieces)
4 pigs trotters
2 kg (4 lb) veal and beef bones
 (preferably marrow bones, sawn
 into pieces)
60 g (2 oz) dripping

2 cups carrots, chopped
2 cups onions, chopped
1½ cups celery, chopped
1 bouquet garni of parsley,
 thyme, majoram
4 bay leaves
12 black peppercorns
24 cups (6 litres) water

1. In a large saucepan, place all ingredients, except the bouquet garni, peppercorns and water and cook gently, stirring occasionally, until the meat, bones and vegetables have browned slightly.
2. Add the bouquet garni and peppercorns.
3. Add the water and slowly bring to the boil.
4. Simmer 6-8 hours until the liquid is reduced to 16 cups (4 litres).
5. Cool and strain through muslin. Skim off the fat by refrigerating the liquid overnight and removing the congealed fat the next day.

Brown Roux

Makes 1 cup (8 fl oz)

125 g (4 oz) butter
¾ cup (3 oz) flour

1. Melt the butter in a heavy-bottomed saucepan.
2. Take it off the heat and, stirring with a wooden spoon or whisk, add the sifted flour. Stir until the mixture is smooth.
3. Return to the heat and, stirring constantly, cook until the roux has a light brown colour.

Sauce Espagnole

This is the basis for many other sauces and it can be refrigerated and deep-frozen for future use.

½ cup bacon, chopped
½ cup carrots, chopped
½ cup onions, chopped
½ cup celery, chopped
1 tablespoon chopped thyme
2 bay leaves

¾ cup (6 fl oz) dry white wine
1 cup (8 fl oz) brown roux
1 cup (8 fl oz) concentrated
 tomato purée
16 cups (4 litres) hot brown meat stock

1. In a large saucepan, fry the bacon, add the vegetables and cook them gently until lightly coloured.
2. Add the thyme and bayleaves.
3. Add the wine, then the roux and stir.
4. Add the tomato purée and gradually stir in the stock, making sure there are no lumps.
5. Stir frequently, while bringing the sauce to the boil, so that it does not stick to the bottom of the saucepan.
6. Place the saucepan on the flame in such a way that it is just under one edge of the saucepan.
7. Simmer 3-4 hours, stirring frequently and occasionally removing the spume which accumulates on the surface on the opposite edge to the flame.
8. The sauce should be completed when it reduces to 8 cups (2 litres) of liquid.
9. Sieve and cover the surface with plastic to prevent formation of a skin.

Demi-glace

Used as a basis for many sauces or to give added body to some sauces.

Makes 2 cups (16 fl oz)

2 cups (16 fl oz) brown meat stock
2 cups (16 fl oz) sauce Espagnole

1. Add the meat stock to the Espagnole and simmer, frequently skimming off the spume.
2. Cook until it reduces to 2 cups.
3. Strain through a fine cloth or sieve. Store in sealed container until ready to use.

Sauce Madère

Madeira sauce

Makes 1 cup (8 fl oz)

3 tablespoons Madeira
1 cup (8 fl oz) beef stock

30 g (1 oz) butter
¼ cup (1 oz) flour

1. Add 1 tablespoon of Madeira to the beef stock and bring it to the boil in a saucepan.
2. In a clean saucepan, melt the butter and add the flour to make a roux.
3. Add the beef stock and Madeira mixture, stirring well with a wire whisk to make a thickened sauce.
4. Simmer gently for a few minutes.
5. Finish the sauce with the remaining 2 tablespoons of Madeira and strain.

Fish Fumet

Fish stock

Makes approximately 1¾ cups (14 fl oz)

1 kg (2 lb) fish trimmings, such as fish
heads, bones, fresh or cooked
shellfish leftovers
1 onion, thinly sliced
6-8 parsley stems (not the leaves; they
will darken the stock)

1 teaspoon lemon juice
¼ teaspoon salt
1 cup (8 fl oz) dry white wine
cold water to cover

1. Place all the ingredients in a large heavy saucepan.
2. Bring it to the boil, skim, and simmer gently for 30 minutes.
3. Strain the stock through a fine sieve and correct the seasoning.
4. Fish stock may be refrigerated or deep frozen.

Pancake Batter

Makes 20-24 pancakes

2 cups (8 oz) flour
1 tablespoon sugar
(for sweet pancakes)
salt

1¾ cups (14 fl oz) milk
3 eggs, beaten
1½ tablespoons melted butter or oil

1. Sift together the flour, sugar and salt.
2. Mix in the milk, eggs and melted butter gradually to avoid lumps.
3. Blend well, then leave to stand for at least 2 hours before cooking.
4. The batter should be as thin as cream. If it looks too thick, add a little water.
5. Grease the pan lightly with butter.
6. For each pancake, spoon about 2 tablespoons of the batter into the heated pan, swirling the pan to allow the batter to thinly coat the entire surface.
7. Brush a piece of butter around the edge of the hot pan with the point of a knife.
8. Cook over a medium heat until just golden but not brown (about 1 minute each side).
9. Repeat until all the pancakes are cooked, stacking them on a plate as they are ready.
10. Cover them with foil to prevent drying out.

Short Crust Pastry

Makes 250 g (8 oz)

2 cups (8 oz) flour
pinch of salt
pinch of sugar

185 g (6 oz) cold butter
a little cold milk

1. Place the flour, salt, sugar and butter in a mixing bowl:
2. Rub the flour and butter together rapidly between the tips of your fingers until the butter is broken into small crumbs.
3. Add the milk and blend quickly with your hand, gathering the dough into a mass.
4. Press the dough into a roughly shaped ball — it should just hold together and be pliable, not damp and sticky.
5. Place the dough on a lightly floured pastry board and knead it gently to ensure a thorough blend of ingredients.
6. Gather it again into a ball, sprinkle it lightly with flour and wrap it in greaseproof paper.
7. Place it in the refrigerator to chill slightly before using.

Puff Pastry

Makes 250 g (8 oz)

2 cups (8 oz) flour
salt
cold water

few drops of lemon juice
220 g (7 oz) butter or margarine

1. Sift the flour and salt together.
2. Mix to a smooth dough with cold water and a few drops of lemon juice.
3. Roll out on a floured board into an oblong shape.
4. Make the butter or margarine into a neat block, and place it in the centre of the pastry.
5. Fold first the bottom section of the pastry over the butter, and then the top section, so that it is quite covered.
6. Turn the dough at right angles, press the edges together and depress it with a rolling pin at intervals, to give a corrugated effect and to equalise the pressure of air.
7. Roll it out to an oblong shape again.
8. Fold the dough into an envelope, turn it, seal it and repeat the above process.
9. Repeat this process five times, making seven rollings and seven foldings in all.
10. Put the pastry in a cold place to prevent it from becoming sticky and soft.
11. Always chill it before rolling it for the last time, and before baking.

Index

151

152